T0329203

POEMS OF THIS WAR

CONTENTS

INTRODUCTION

The poetry written during the War of 1914–1918 and inspired or modified by that War was various enough, but could be divided mainly into two classes. There was the work of the veteran authors, such as Hardy, Kipling, Stephen Phillips, and some who happily are still with us; and there was the expression of the young and often unknown writers, who were called in a general way the Soldier Poets. From the older men, especially at the outset, we heard characteristic utterances. As time went on, we found a deepening interest in the imparted feelings and perceptions of those on whom the intense experience had fallen most urgently. Not the least impressive thing was to discover how many of that war generation had relied upon verse as a way of reflecting intimately and independently. Far more of them practised poetry than published it themselves or even divulged it to a friend in some interval between the immediate tasks of active service.

Parallels between the two Wars are to be drawn with reserve. But here in the third year of the new World War an anthology appears which brings out the impression made lately by other evidences. It tells us that this time as last, war has not silenced the Muses in England armed and embattled. Young men and women are responding to what is happening to themselves and to humanity at large in the terms, symbols and logic of poetry. Not all of the writers assembled by Miss Ledward and Mr Strang, I suppose—for the majority of the contributors are personally unknown to me—are engaged in active service; but all represent the generation which particularly comes face to face with war. The reader who is eager to know something more of the present than he can readily find in the day's round will mark what these soldier poets have to say; our consideration of it will perhaps be most thoughtful where their matter, impulse, declared or implied judgment varies from the mass of things circulated in time of war.

For now, as at all periods, and especially when the peace-time allurements of literary reputation, social reward and the rest of Vanity Fair are out of season, poetry is written because its principle is one of 'the innocent eye'. Its mood is that of seeing where the truth is, or recording things observed and apprehended which may open the way thither. The poets do not necessarily agree with one another, nor must they be always in one mood; this may be seen in the following pages. One writer may tell us,

> All Nature's agents image war to me.
> Even that butterfly above the ditch
> Flutters with sinister intent; a bee,
> Heavy with honey, drones at bomber's pitch....

Another finds the same infection of all things lovely:

> I tread
> The white dust of a weed-bright lane; alone
> Upon Time-Present's tranquil outmost rim,
> Seeing the sunlight through a lens of dread,
> While anguish makes the English landscape seem
> Inhuman as the jungle, and unreal
> Its peace.

Yet to a third a missel-thrush's song is still quite a cheerful and untroubled performance:

> No thought of rationing or raid
> Occurred to mar his serenade,
> And politicians were to him,
> I knew, superfluous and grim.
> He honed his beak for an encore;
> He cared no whit about the war.

There is a theme on which, I believe, these poets are in accord; it is one of joy, though set against a background of fiery shadow. Not long ago the god of love was becoming something of a scarecrow, but the error has been admitted. The young poets are with Robert Burns so far as this subject is concerned. They have done with analytical approaches and consultations, and they speak clearly and universally:

> I know that in my mind
> You stay when others pass,
> And entering a room
> The sun is in your face.

Or again,

> Now in this quiet hour, listening to traffic,
> While the sun sways us and the music hovers
> Over this tragic season: while the guns
> Boom on over the continent, I see
> Amply the simple movement of our love.

As a series of thoughts upon the War in its relation to the lives and ardours of the writers, the poems do not easily yield to one definition; possibly 'In Time of Suspense' (p. 11) portrays in the fullest way the new generation meeting the new breaking of nations. Neither in that nor in any other of the poems is there any militarism, or personal claim, or study of revenge. There is not even much irony, though disenchantment finds a voice:

> When I was a civilian I hoped high,
> Dreamt my future cartwheels in the sky,
> Almost forgot to arm myself
> Against the boredom and the inefficiency
> The petty injustice and the everlasting grudges.
> The sacrifice is greater than I ever expected.

To measure the time deliberately is for some a way past disenchantment:

ix

So now, leaning against my gun, in these fields and
Plains of Belgium, conscious of the warp and fret
Of spring on the hedges and forests, I accept! I accept!

For there lies all our power; the power of the young and
the lonely.
I know that the past is lies, and the present only
Important. I see in life service, and in dying an end
Of loving.

The way in which war saps at the treasured conquests of
the human spirit is occasionally exposed:

In nature class the schoolboy's head
is taught to contemplate, instead
of flower pot and cactus stump,
a budding aluminium dump.

The chances, the prospect, are touched upon, but without
elaborate protest:

After the band has gone
There will be music
But how many of us will be there to hear it?

Through all, sparing as are the allusions to the actual
ordeals of individuals, I feel the burden of their fate. The
music of the verses it may be, that conveys something
more than the details in the words; or, as to the things
notified in the words, perhaps it is from the things which
are not mentioned and which lie beyond the stanzas
written that the profounder emotion is stirred. Here a
brief reference to the technical side of the poems in
general may be in place. We have witnessed in the years
before the war a great deal of revolutionary ingenuity
in the writing of poetry, and may have thought it was
wasted. It had the look of being done chiefly because
the inventors were determined to avoid beaten tracks,
and escape the epithet 'literary'. If we say that it was
metrical and idiomatic experiment, its transitory character

is still in our minds. But in respect of the informal and sketch-like pieces which the present volume contains, that reflection does not arise. The growth is natural and proper to the strained circumstances. All the polishing in the world would not increase, indeed would impair, the fresh and significant appeal of these songs of emergency. The question of their being called 'literary' or not did not trouble their writers, who had just time to leave a word with us before the column was moving off once more:

> All this shall pass,
> But this shall be again,...
> Peace enters singly as she always came
> When she desired Eternal rest:
> It is her singleness impressed
> Upon a soul, a soul, a soul,
> That shall in time give wisdom to the whole.

In the end, as with the poetry of that other War, the striking thing about this anthology is the separate ways the poets have taken and the singleness of temper and trust which they achieve. Within the narrow limits which each inevitably receives in such a collection, it is not possible to consider them as we have been enabled to consider Brooke, Sorley, F. W. Harvey, Sassoon, Owen and others whose distinct writings formed at length the poetic truth of the earlier conflict. But they in their turn, speaking in solitariness, contribute to a sensitive and honourable interpretation of the difficult as well as deadly problem of these years. It is not the least of England's titles to eminence that so many of her sons and daughters, in the midst of the most exacting and devastating changes of fortune, can view life through the medium of poetry, and 'gently take that which ungently came'. As a member of another generation I conceive it to be a great privilege to have been admitted thus to a private world of incident, sympathy and philosophy which in real life might have been long hidden by shyness or want of conversational eloquence; and it seems to me that all who are anxious to explore the meaning of the present and to understand those on whom the future depends will find valuable enlightenment here, and only in such pages as these.

EDMUND BLUNDEN

1942

I. *'We saw doom patterned in the ordinary sky'*

I. THE CONSCRIPTS

We go to war in various ways
From farms and factories, the usual ways
Of life suddenly distorted to terrible
Experience. Thus fear becomes the visible
Coffin at the funeral.

We saw doom patterned in the ordinary sky.
Here we go who yesterday
Were the people, the men who are to be
The people after the whirlpool stills
And quiet regains the valleys and the hills.

These were the neighbours
Of our fear, theirs was the curse
As well. The prophecy ran coldly
In our common blood and cried loudly
For swift sacrifice.

We saw doom patterned in the ordinary sky.
After all there was a universal
Tongue waiting patiently to assemble
The unmarshalled needs. Who sought to leap
Alone are marching now in step.

We go to war in various ways
Yet each aspires above himself to raise
The defeated banners. We have broken our fear.
The hour explodes the familiar life: we bear
The bleeding memory on.

We see birth patterned in the deathly sky.

EMMANUEL LITVINOFF

2. THOUGHTS ON THE EVE

I could love Life the more
Would it but pass away
As quietly as the day
Ebbs from the darkening star.

This dearly cherished thought,
Deep and enraptured pain,
Soothes like a gentle rain
My wild tempestuous heart.

To sail a billowing sea
And watch the departing shore
From a tall sea-girt tower
Is to die splendidly.

But to my chosen end
I would more humbly creep
As men weary for sleep
Pray darkness descend.

But should some savage Hand
My rising manhood stem,
Torn, haunted by its dream,
From Time, lonely to stand;

Life had I loved the more
Had it but passed away
As quietly as the day
Ebbs from the darkening star.

EMMANUEL LITVINOFF

3. COME! LET US DANCE

Come! let us dance
    The dance of death!
Dissemble doom
    With love's light breath!

Pipe away
  To the metal moon
That hears unmoved
  Our witless tune.

Pluck the lyre
  In a funeral dirge:
We face unswerving
  Death's dread purge;

Dauntless, despotic,
  Devilish, drear,
The purge of death
  Is coming near;

The purge that leaves
  Nor king nor fool
Nor measures man
  By any rule,

But takes us all
  In any order
By heart disease
  Or front-page murder!

Dance, dance
  To the beggar's lute.
Dance, and sing
  Ere he strike you mute.

Come to the dance!
  The dance of death!
Dissemble doom
  With love's light breath!

PETER BAKER

4. THE LEVEL MIND

The level mind bodingly watches
the green leaf that the wrinkle touches—
across young lands the brown leaf marches.

The streets weep, grey and fearing
their memory's sons, summer's bearing—
their heartless foil cold puppets wearing.

Dead plants in honeymoon gardens fallen,
seeds still remembering the vain pollen—
bodies that march, their voices stolen.

The level mind bodingly watches
the fraud hand that the slim life snatches,
the streets that weep the children's marches.

ALEX COMFORT

5. EMPTY SHELLS

I

The red hands took you; to the hot dust beyond
the cool village walks, climbing, riding in rain
past Druid stones, cows at the moorland pond;
kicks at the beech leaves in the lonely lane.
Gorse fired from hill to hill; the golden curl
of cloud; sea-walls cracking, the lean winds flashing
knives of foam to our throats; but you heard
the straining gates where fiercer waves were crashing.

Discussions in cold blood, meetings, delay;
your bag packed, handshakes, everyone away.

I watch the sea-gulls, white screams round the plough;
walk out to the low tide over the red
sand, crush empty shells, thinking of Spain, how
I grow old, and you perhaps are dead.

4

Some thing of Spring in Autumn, of brooding
on change; a deepened music in the skies,
sun striking new chords from the organ earth, moving
deep harmonies in the sea; the woods are wise.

Only our dreams are real—the leaves are dust
where we walked; now, in the blank-staring street,
for those who wait, no answer, only rust
on the clutched rails, and the tread of wearied feet.

The cold dawn, aching; in the numb rain,
lonely travellers in the crowded train.

No strain for hoping now; I can reach
to stillness, with eyes Janus-like at last.
But in empty shells, picked up on the beach,
murmurs the storm to come, the storm past.

MARGARET CROSLAND

6. WAR

Because the world is falling and there comes no answer;
Because the leaves soon hide an outworn age;
Because the time is past for children's playing,
And a stranger suddenly walks upon the stage;
Because the world is not the world we lived in
And life is not a game,
And most of the Gods we worshipped lost their haloes
When the muses lost their name,
We would remember the old days and their imagined
    glories;
The tinsel trappings of a wondrous past.
Postulating that the new world shall be born now
And that this war is the last.

And we would hope that something should be altered
In the cruel careless fundamental law,
But we must beware or the moment will escape us;
It has done so before,
And we must see that out of the practical slaughter
Rise no mere vapoury dreams,
But a world where the poor are fed, the tyrants humbled
And men know what life means.

JOCK CURLE

7. NEWS OF SUFFERING

Shouldering a way through crowds,
Or brooding with the dance of leaf
Delightful on the sunlit page,
I freeze in grief

For trees that will not bud in Spring
Now murder drags faith from its bed,
And the potential serpent coils
In the stern head,

But know my sorrow will not ease
Eyes empty in the last despair:
For me now are the claws of love,
And the sick prayer.

CLIFFORD DYMENT

8. METROPOLIS

I dreamt that suddenly the metropolitan sky
Closed in its dark dome a million dead,
Blindly and soundlessly, merciless like lead,
Shut in a huge tomb that company
Of mad imperial men. I heard their cry

Fade as the door closed, and as the stone
Rolled on their lust and laughter I saw
One most beautifully spared like Noah
Reaching towards me. His blood and bone
Through a pellucid miraculous prism shone.

'I am Shakespeare', he said, and then I knew
How Hamlet hung like a vision in his eye,
Questioning my right to live or die:
Lear and Othello in a storm of dew
Whose passion and tragedy we travel to.

'I too am Christ.' His lips were red
With the bitter vinegar he'd rinsed thereon.
O like a classical bird his heart bore on
My fate like an omen. 'I come', he said,
'With Calvary's disaster on my head.'

Strange in a dream, alone with that man, I stood
At the world's centre, while east and west
Winds worried the nostril of each beast,
The sun shone, birds hopped, leaves of the wood
Lay embalmed in an unreal solitude.

'Shakespeare and Christ, the bright and brittle blade
That splinters with power the city sky,
This is the nerve you live and labour by.'
I remembered the huge tomb, its million dead,
'O what of those mad imperious men?' I said,

And woke. And suddenly the metropolitan sky
Broke in a thousand fragments. I heard
Shakespeare shouting his innumerable word
Louder and louder—the creed, curse, cry
Of men in history.

JOHN HALL

9. CONSCRIPTS

Related to the picnic in the wood,
The letters that the lover failed to post,
    To August, and the closing of the year,
    No formula can exorcise their fear.

Tomorrow stalks the country of their pleasure
And misconstrues the need for sacrifice;
    Because they grudge the summer that they give,
    Our glib memorials are no palliative.

Shipwrecked, they grope forever underseas
Or plot the graph of human recollection.
    Here, on a mountain-range they did not know,
    They see the future buried under snow.

To some, a window set above the park
Affords a passage to their common love;
    As retribution for the cancelled hours,
    Imagination gives the actress flowers.

Others must loiter in the ruined house,
Knees flexed above a phantom of the mind,
    Or let the demon lead them to the street;
    For them love's currency is counterfeit.

Recoiling from the certainty of touch,
They write their passion in another's book:
    The rhyme and reason of the present tense
    Is found in motion or impermanence.

In privacy they play their own Iago,
And juggle with the language of the flesh;
    Because pretence and disbelief are one,
    They fear the revelation of the sun.

Shall they return to find the garden empty,
And sweep the cobwebs from an upstairs room?
    See, in the wounded mirror on the wall,
    The anger of the present shadows all.

FRANCIS KING

10. GONE IS THE SPRING

Gone is the spring, and the undertones
of summer, heavy and ominous, demanding
from the living life, from the dead that their ageless
        shadow
obscure not the sickening lie which haunts the pages of
        history.

Now let us simplify the issue,
canalizing moods and currents which fox us
into believing this or doing that, irrespective
of the long insistent desire to thatch our untented houses.

Weaving our dreams of folly and delight, or
examining with microscopic glance
the fears and visions of childhood, the conditional
        WHY of
events which suddenly shamed our pretty, unwanted
        endearments.

'We too have demands of a rational nature,
we guests to your dream kingdom;
for we have our claim, our honour; your hidden anger
cannot relieve you now: we are not very impressed
with your ancient sport of the ostrich, the power and the
subtlety of the seashell's wished-for music,
sharpening the bronze voices of boys, and their waiting
bodies, the hopes and desire of their graceful, desolate
        movements.'

The cant of reactionary, forget it!
Renounce now the plaint of children, with their
stupid, lovable faces and futile regrets, for
theirs is the sensitive withdrawal, the studied retreat
        of the snail

or the cannon. For you is memory and magic,
power of limb and the possible forgiveness.
Say 'For us to act, and action is loving—that,
and the silent faith to unite with life, ignored by the
  selfish.'

Because hatred is power, and impotence
suffering, to idle death to the living,
what then? Shall we say the link, the long and magical
chain of history is broken, the umbilical cord is severed?

And so on this summer evening the voices
of saints, and the prayer of the small and the lonely
shall be our questioners, and the silent face of memory
our accuser; the song of the helpless our history, and
  our answer.

ALAN ROOK

II. SEPTEMBER HOLIDAY

All Nature's agents image war to me.
Even that butterfly above the ditch
Flutters with sinister intent; a bee,
Heavy with honey, drones at bomber's pitch.
The distant tractor furrows for attack
Trenches meticulous as a general's plan.
Those corn-shocks rest like rifles in a stack;
That sheaf ungathered is a fallen man . . .
Nothing is simple now, nothing immune
From war's contagion, time's conspiracy.
Throughout the sunny Cotswold afternoon
All Nature's agents image death to me.

CLIVE SANSOM

12. IN TIME OF SUSPENSE

Draw-to the curtains then, and let it rain.
We'll look no more on that disordered scene:
Blind rage upon a blinded window-pane,
The shivering white upon the darkening green;
Nor that beyond it leaping to and fro,
Ghost in the ruined garden, or mad briar.
Shut out confusion, draw the curtains to,
Build the cathedrals of the fire anew.
Close, eyes, on doubt, and open on desire.

Here, in the quiet brilliance of belief,
We fashion life at such intensity,
The very chairs might rustle into leaf
And panels grope to build their primal tree.
Now when our bodies meet like star and star,
Now when our minds remoter commerce do,
No wish too subtle and no world too far,
But we, so perfectly in tune we are,
Passionately conceive and make it true.

And so farewell to Winter, for I hear
The lambs rejoicing on a hill of jade,
The blackbird in his vocal graph of fear
Scattering darkness down the painted glade.
It crowds the curtains, mad in bud and wing,
That world of passion that your fancy craves,
That England that the fancy, quickening,
Cannot but call the very eye of Spring,
Lashed by the curled abandon of her waves!

Folly of dreaming, when you have entwined
Wild arms about the dreamer and the dream!
Drawn by those gentle Avons I shall find
A land where April does not merely seem.

11

Narrow horizons! Yet how wide to me
For whom they compass all those island charms
That I must die to safeguard, it may be:
An England the aspiring candles see,
Narrow enough to compass in my arms.

So in this room. But when I stood alone
One evening on a windy crown of land
Beneath the emblem of a youthful moon,
And watched oblivion like a tired hand
Folding the map of Spring away, I knew
Hill upon hill receding were no more
Than picture and faint effigy of you,
Nor shall I ever after lose that view
Though I descend into the night of war.

For us, no heartening slogan will assuage
What must be suffered in the mad descent.
We dreamed that war was but an awkward age
And country could be lost in continent.
The cretin world remains where it began,
Clings to the shambles and improvement shelves.
Too undeceived for patriotic man
Youth takes up arms to rescue what it can;
For all is lost but what we have ourselves.

When war came to our cradles once, it meant
Only the mutter of a thunder-clap
Somewhere beyond the tidy hills of Kent,
A black line every morning on a map,
Germans in the allotment, trains unlit—
Did we not learn of war in gentle doses?
We merely breathed it like a dangerous grit
In every breath we drew, contracted it
From our warm bottles like tuberculosis.

Formed by the years of agony, wherein
Fear stole into the heart and set up house,
Formed to be nervous as a violin,
We find no brothers in the dead. For us
No voice will speak in the white cemeteries
Of France. We are not of that careless kind
To whom life seemed to offer prize on prize,
Who, at the terminus, with laughing eyes
Saw only joy in battle. Blind, stark blind.

Nor are we of the next unhappy age
That laughed, with laughter hollow as an urn
Raised to belief, the murdered heritage.
Now from those ageing pantaloons we learn
The young are very serious. Even so.
As passionately serious as the Spring
After the sterile gaieties of snow.
Give us but time enough, and we will show
These barren valleys how to laugh and sing!

Give us but time, we say. For now, on all,
The radiant anguish of a dream is thrown.
Vivid the bird beyond the orchard wall
Who fills Goodnight with poignancy unknown.
More beautiful because it is more haunted
Our world revolves. Accusing as a text,
These walls, these shapes of love we have been granted,
Are critically watching though enchanted:
'This Winter, yes', they nod at us. 'But next?'

Thus for the island genius, Liberty,
Much loved by Roman letters in our stone,
Another generation learns to die
Gravely, not caring if the flags are flown,

13

Believing simply it must save for Earth
A way of life becoming to mankind,
A grace of centuries, a thing of worth:
This we believe, who by a peaceful hearth
Have laughing eyes tonight, but are not blind.

Then let the violin on its own nerves
Be racked, if only the sweet Master seek
The harmony its brittle heart conserves.
What if, while you and I contrive to speak
With exiled April in a distant room,
The clouds should lift, and a young moon outside
Swim like an amulet beyond the gloom?
Shall we not look upon this night to come?
Blow out the candles—throw the curtains wide!

LAURENCE WHISTLER

II. 'Line after line, we wheel to enter battle'

13. LINE AFTER LINE

Line after line, we wheel to enter battle;
Soon, above the cannonry, we'll hear
Death's rattle;
Our life is short, a mound of earth our shrine,
But others went to die, and showed no fear,
Line after line.

We cannot pause to think of life or death,
Until the final, fatal cannonade
Tests the faith
That once held firm to universal laws;
In this dread hour, but one law we have made.
We cannot pause.

PETER BAKER

14. WHAT I NEVER SAW

I was ready for death,
Ready to give my all in one expansive gesture
For a cause that was worthy of death.
I wanted to fear, to watch blood and torture,
To draw my last breath
Amidst a chaos of dramatic thunder.
I dreamt of aeroplanes sweeping the sky,
Gave war her ghastly lure,
Came, ready to fight and to die.

I thought in my mufti
Of brave men marching to battle
And came here to join them,
To share the machine guns' rattle.

15

What I never saw
Were the weary hours of waiting while the sun rose
    and set,
The everlasting eye turned upwards to the sky
Watching the weather which said,
'Thou shalt not fly.'

We sat together as we sat at peace
Bound by no ideal of service
But by a common interest in pornography and a desire to
    outdrink one another.
War was remote:
There was a little trouble in Abyssinia;
Some of us came from Kenya and said
'Why I was on the spot all the while
And the Italians sprayed the roadsides with mustard gas.'
Theirs were the stories of war.

Then came the queuing, the recurrent line of pungent
    men
Dressed in dirt with mud eating their trouser legs,
The collar that is cleaner than the shirt
And the inevitable adjectives.

The papers ran out early today,
There was no butter for the bread at breakfast,
Nobody calls us at dawn,
We never strain or sweat,
Nor do they notice when we come in late.

When I was a civilian I hoped high,
Dreamt my future cartwheels in the sky,
Almost forgot to arm myself
Against the boredom and the inefficiency
The petty injustice and the everlasting grudges.
The sacrifice is greater than I ever expected.

TIMOTHY CORSELLIS

15. THE TEMPLE

Luke tells us how Jesus
Was missed on the return to Galilee:
He had tarried in the Temple, zealous to learn
What his Father's will was to be.

I think of this page in Luke now.
I have left the soldiery to march ahead
And I lie here, the hawthorn budding,
The celandines like stars about my head.

This morning I surprised a stoat
Feasting on the blood of a hare;
And now, all around me, the wedding songs of birds
Blossom in the air.

I ponder: some million years ago
Forests and crying fearful beasts perished
When a sea shuddered and threw up a mountain
To make this hill on which I rest.

Must death create? I speak
My question in this Temple under the sky—
But no answer comes from stoat or bird or hill
Whether it is man's Cross to kill, or die.

CLIFFORD DYMENT

16. MAN AND BEAST

Hugging the ground by the lilac tree,
With shadows in conspiracy,

The black cat from the house next door
Waits with death in each bared claw

For some tender unwary bird
That all the summer I have heard

In the orchard singing. I hate
The cat that is its savage fate,

And choose a stone with which to end
This menace to my woodland friend.

I look to where the black cat lies,
But drop my stone, seeing its eyes—

Who is it sins now, those eyes say,
You the hunter, or I, the prey?

CLIFFORD DYMENT

17. THE UNCERTAIN BATTLE

Away the horde rode, in a storm of hail
And steel-blue lightning. Hurtled by the wind
Into their eardrums from behind the hill
Came in increasing bursts the startled sound
Of trumpets in the unseen hostile camp.—
Down through a raw black hole in heaven stared
The horror-blanched moon's eye. Across the swamp
Five ravens flapped; and the storm disappeared
Soon afterwards, like them, into that pit
Of Silence which lies waiting to consume
Even the braggart World itself at last....
The candle in the hermit's cave burned out
At dawn, as usual.—No-one ever came
Back down the hill, to say which side had lost.

DAVID GASCOYNE

18. LEST YOU FORGET

When the toll is heavy,
the harsh hours taut with suffering,
and the nights, the long desolate nights,
bleakly mock the grief in your heart,
remember they, too, have cried out in anguish,
and tear up the rank weeds of bitterness
lest they turn the garden of your soul
into a wilderness.

When the flesh you cherished
for its sweetness has vanished like smoke,
when the strong thighs you made wise to passion
have died in the delirium of violence,
when there is only darkness in eyes you loved
for their light and you cannot recall the sound
of a lost voice,
when silence is ugly and laughter is pain,.
remember the others who beat their hopeless breasts
lest your sacrifice be in vain.

And in the slow days of forgetting
when the mutilated members of your soul
put forth new buds,
and the earth you once thought barren forever
grows fertile from your tears
yielding new treasures unto the morrow,
remember the others for the fresh hope they know
lest your joy turn to grief again.

EMMANUEL LITVINOFF

19. SOLDIER'S DEATH

He stopped—hit! The ground reeled and smacked his
    face;
He cried; light burst and splintered in his brain,
Blackness collapsed in halls of breaking glass,
Pain was life's last joke, the god he knew then;
His fingers fumbled, tried still harder, groped
For touch, and failed; all feeling, faithful things,
Escaping and confused, cheated and mocked
The dying man; harder he pulled the strings
Of frozen senses, could no longer find
His hands and feet, found nothing but the blind
Of dying; hard he sought for that great prize,

The power of life itself, the right of breath,
Till, queerly, quietly he relaxed. Was peace
Rewarded, some slight pause? Or was this death
The final verdict? Was this end complete,
This worthless crumpled breakdown, this defeat?

KENNETH NEAL

20. HALE, Y.M.C.A.

(Written on returning from Christmas leave)

The piano vaguely strums old tunes,
Across the smoke and talk recalls
A moment, multiplies a memory, dies and falls
Then changes partners, leaves Atlantis in our arms,
And all for nothing. I thought here is Freud and Adler,
Here the unrehearsed familiarity of soldiers
Grows, thickens, develops an eternity, becomes
Important, a parcel of the afternoon.
Here the welcome of cigarettes and tea,
The firm handshake of hearty laughter,
The familiarity of things we understand.

Outside the exiled wind grumbles round the door
And winter's edge sharpens the corners
Of the evening, bitterly but honestly;
Inside we take the edge off life itself,
Do nothing, think, gaze at the past, endure
Ourselves, suffer our neighbours,
Let jealousy grow dangerous fingers,
Eat, do everything, commit adultery by proxy—
(The shawl has fallen from her shoulders
And she slips into her bed)—
All this before the afternoon is dead,
All this and more, while one man fumbles
For his matches, and another yawns.

Last week's Christmas hung across the room,
Drooping from the ceiling, dispirited,
Reminds us another Christmas is gone
And what have we achieved, what done?
They go on, the smoke and the talk,
The piano and the soldiers,
The soldiers let the piano take them for a walk,
But what will be achieved or won?

KENNETH NEAL

21. ARMY

Tomorrow and tomorrow and tonight,
Remorselessly the useless hours pass by
Without a pause: Old Time is sitting tight,
And men live here to learn to kill and die;
And day decays, slowly, meanly, falls
Into that well the living call the past
Like paper peeling from neglected walls.
Let us have some clean killing at the last!
We're tired of waste and muddle and the mind
Perpetually and helplessly confined
To barracks and parades upon a tidy square:
It's mad—the stupid and the humble folk
Are khaki heroes here, the beautiful's a swear
Word and our lives a dirty joke.

KENNETH NEAL

22. EARLY MORNING

The dawn's a dirty smudge of light
Advancing westwards as night's troops retreat;
The soldiers sleep; some shovelled into huts,
Some clustered up in concrete forts,
And rifles rest beside each trusting head,
And great guns guard the living and the dead;
A late star seems quite humorous and gay
And young light gleams upon the bayonet point.

So still and quiet—a stir would be a curse,
A rash leaf disturb the universe.
And while the soldiers sleep, beneath the boards
The rats run random riot, steal and squeak,
Indulge their natures like unlovely lords
And play the freedom of the beast.

The bugle call; broken the bloodshot dawn.
The bugle call; the soldier licks away the taste
Of sleep, wiping from yawning eyes the waste
Of dreams; then, pushing back rest's blanket
With rest that's still unfinished, leaves
In unprotected corners of his heart
The gathered forces of subconscious griefs.

And so the wheels are made to start;
A curse and cough are terms to greet the day
And mend the man to march into the morn
And send him with a swagger from the barrack-room.

With tramp of troops and tread of boots
The day parades on time; the sun
Is never out of step but grimly foots
Along in his allotted rank in some
Huge army marching to its doom,
And as the Army keeps in step
One soldier thinks:—there once was war
But now there're only oaths and drill:
Another:—blind my brain and bare,
Heavy my helmet head and dumb my mind,
Left, right, left, right, left, left, left:
A third:—my boots bite the ground and grind
My back, I know not how to kill,
I remember when I saw a kitten die:
Left, right, left, right, left, left, left:
A fourth:—these steps will never cease,
Down generations they have trod,
And every step asks why, why, why are these

Young men drawn up in lines as straight
As rifle fire when sights are accurate;
Another:—at home there's still my wife
But now I've been a soldier all my life:
Another:—how safe and gentle is the sky,
How tragic that there is no God.

KENNETH NEAL

23. CLEATOR MOOR

From one shaft at Cleator Moor
They mined for coal and iron ore.
This harvest below ground could show
Black and red currants on one tree.

In furnaces they burnt the coal,
The ore they smelted into steel,
And railway lines from end to end
Corseted the bulging land.

Pylons sprouted on the fells,
Stakes were driven in like nails,
And the ploughed fields of Devonshire
Were sliced with the steel of Cleator Moor.

The land waxed fat and greedy too,
It would not share the fruits it grew,
And coal and ore, as sloe and plum,
Lay black and red for jamming time.

The pylons rusted on the fells,
The gutters leaked beside the walls,
The women searched the ebb-tide tracks
For knobs of coal and broken sticks.

But now the pits are wick with men,
Digging like dogs dig for a bone:
For food and life *we* dig the earth—
In Cleator Moor they dig for death.

Every waggon of cold coal
Is fire to drive a turbine wheel;
Every knuckle of soft ore
A bullet in a soldier's ear.

The miner at the rockface stands,
With his segged and bleeding hands
Heaps on his head the fiery coal,
And feels the iron in his soul.

NORMAN NICHOLSON

24. THE RETREAT

Faint now behind the secret eyes of these
The sleepers, the dreamers, the exact and delicate
Flowering of our age, dusk steals. And over

The trees and rivers, over the golden meadows and
    vines the glow
Of death is spreading. I one with them
Feel the pulse stir strangely. Now

Evening introduces her sudden crisis
Of vermilion and shadows. Silence falls
Over the cultivated secrecy of these faces.

I too with these have suffered. I too have felt
The richness pass and the inexplicable beauty
Of memory fading—lost in the present. Defeat,

Humiliation, and the dreaded tremendous excitement
Of movement and change were ours, in our blood, our
    fever.
Not alone in the aeroplane or the shell, not confined

To the trickery and lies, the treacherous bullet. No,
But even in fellowship, the touch of hand, in the quiet
Word, in the eyes of a daisy, or the timelessness of trees
Lies fear. Death haunts the flowers and cities.

So now, leaning against my gun, in these fields and
Plains of Belgium, conscious of the warp and fret
Of spring on the hedges and forests, I accept! I accept!

For there lies all our power; the power of the young and
    the lonely.
I know that the past is lies, and the present only
Important. I see in life service, and in dying an end

Of loving. I know that the evil in our nature
Is our fear of history, our incapacity to suffer,
And our poor cold dread of the crises of the future.

The sun bows. And now the earth, the mother,
Is cold. The patient suffering of these my friends, their
Lucid sorrow, is my burden and my song.

ALAN ROOK

25.   ON GUARD

The hush of waves reminds me of my love
And the small stars that are so bright
        To relieve the horror we all face,
        Making a loneliness at night.

Remember me as you lie in bed
With thoughts perhaps that were once shared;
        At this hour a shadow seems
        Your ghost when I feel tired.

I did not think a year ago
That parting could be so complete;
        Each single hour you're worlds away
        I feel alone and separate.

Now living wears the look of death
And all our dreams are growing old;
        Should we have seen the end, my dear?
        It was not heart that first grew cold.

JOHN WALLER

III. 'After the sirens sound'

26. AIR-RAID WARNING

After the sirens sound, the air
Is strangely still, as though its breath
Were taken from it by despair
At children joining hands with death.
The gusty laughter in the street
Is switched off like a broken tune
As through the air there comes the beat
Of distant bombers, while the sky
Which knows the ageless sun and moon,
The secrets of each wind and tide,
Looks down on man's stupidity,
A world committing suicide,
With sad all-seeing eye.

DOUGLAS GIBSON

27. CELLAR

These faces—the cold apples in a loft
huddled in rows, each shining green
catching a convex light, under the grey rat's foot
impotent, are not so quiet—

grey faces, hollow where the wasps
have been at them, after the fungus, turnip lanterns
are not so empty, impartial between self
and the small house under the imminent thunder.

26

These do not vary as the mind flickers—
blue hollows under jaws, shadows on throats—
not knowing, lying as apples lie
listening to the rat coming through the paper.

Only in this quiet, this hot listening, we hear
the hiss of stars in the river, going out.

ALEX COMFORT

28. THE POOR AT WAR
    (Britain, winter 1940)

O that one current steady across years!—
Millions, millions of arms forever reaching,
Athwart the saint's example and his teaching,
Backwards from poverty, away from tears!

These many now for righteousness and good
Enduring terrors, anguish, mutilations,
Leave the one-way and nameless generations,
Live with that lovable small multitude
Who, their simple hearths and suppers calling,
Stayed on the fells far off as dusk was falling,
Eating up every word the prophet said,
Dimly aware that such alone could save them—
Who were amazed when tenderly he gave them,
After that feast, the meal of fish and bread.

N. K. CRUICKSHANK

29. AIR RAID

Whenever I am sad because of news
That shocks my eyes in headlines,
I only have to think of you to want to sing.
Walking in stores where gas suits are for sale
(Deadly among the stockings and the flasks of scent)
I am reminded of your talk of frocks,
Instead of grieving at the sound of shells.

Love, and not hate, is a cause for pride,
Love is the Prince of valiant people—
And so I am not shamed if I am moved
To remember the night of flame and metal,
Not by the searchlights harassing the stars,
Nor by the loud bomber lurking in the clouds,
But by the image of your sweet scared face
That had no hauteur then, its long desire
Vivid and wordless in the flares.   CLIFFORD DYMENT

30.   HEDGEHOG IN AIR RAID

The sky was a terrific beach
From which the sea had crawled,
Leaving behind lakes of cool pellucid light,
Masses of indigo and sepia cloud,
Wrack strewn and piled, and brilliance
Shooting off the waters
Rippling because of the wind.

I stood on the edge of the beach,
A single watcher in a distance no eye could measure:

And marvelled at the night, its tranquillity,
At the night, its terror—

For the night was tranquil and terrible enough
Without man
Slipping like a shark through the seas,
Pale belly lit by the moon,
Jaw ripe for ripping and blood.

I lifted my eyes to the scene of the beach.
In the huge night alone,
Aghast at the grandeur of the night,
My heart was painful for love of the world—
Horror and joy, frail and strong,
The hill and the poised bird,
Buildings, people with words on their lips—
For these, the world, I was in pain.

Over the grass a hedgehog came
Questing the air for scents of food
And the cracked twig of danger.
He shuffled near in the gloom. Then stopped.
He was aware of me. I went up,
Bent low to look at him, and saw
His coat of lances pointing to my hand.
What could I do
To show I was no enemy?
I turned him over, inspected his small clenched paws,
His eyes expressionless as glass,
And did not know how I could speak,
By tongue or touch, the language of a friend.

It was a grief, to be a friend
Yet to be dumb; to offer peace
And bring the soldiers out.

I went aside, stood still to think of a way:
Then soon the hedgehog stirred, lurching off in haste,
Taking away a friend perhaps,
Taking away a fear
That what seems sweet will poison,
That what seems gentle, pierce.

In the whole of the night, nothing
To heal my sorrow. Only the shark in the skies
To mend my grief.

I offered love, but found no language;
I offered love, but was not trusted;
I offered peace, but brought the soldiers out.

I lifted my eyes to the scene of the beach,
Where the shark hunted out in the seas,
Where the light shot off the lakes.

CLIFFORD DYMENT

On Sundays friends arrive with kindly words
To peer at those whom war has crushed;
They bring the roar of health into these hushed
And solemn wards—
The summer wind blows through the doors and cools
The sweating forehead; it revives
Memories of other lives
Spent lying in the fields, or by sea-pools;
And ears that can discern
Only the whistling of a bomb it soothes
With tales of water splashing into smooth
Deep rivers fringed with ferns.
Nurses with level eyes, and chaste
In long starched dresses, move
Amongst the maimed, giving love
To strengthen bodies gone to waste.
The convalescents have been wheeled outside,
The sunshine strikes their cheeks and idle fingers,
Bringing to each a sensuous languor
And sentimental sorrow for the dead.

Over the human scene stands the old castle, its stone
Now tender in the sun; even the gargoyles seem to
    find
Some humour in the vision of mankind
Lying relaxed and helplessly alone.
Only the Tudor Roses view with grief
The passing of a kingly age,
The dwindling of a history page,
False-faced religion, sham belief.

Six—the clock chimes for the visitors to go:
The widow reading to her son shuts up the book,
The lover takes his final look

At the mutilated face, so bravely gay;
The young wife, with husband full of shot,
Kisses his brow and quickly walks away,
Her eyes on the stalwart boughs that sway
Still seeing the flatness of his sheets;
The child with dark curls, beloved of all the others,
Jingles his coins and waves bare feet,
Like lily petals, to entreat
One penny more from his departing brother.

One by one the wards empty, happiness goes,
The hospital routine, the usual work
Return for another week;
The patients turn upon themselves, a hundred foes
Imagined swell their suffering;
Fretfully hands pick at sheets
And voices meet
Discussing symptoms and the chance of living.
Only the soldier lies remote and resolutely sane,
Remembering how, a boy, he dreamt of folk
With footballs. Maturity dispelled the dream—he woke
To know that he would never walk again.

PATRICIA LEDWARD

32. SEE THE WASTED CITIES!

O see the wasted cities by morning
When the bombers have gone,
See them after moonlight and the unheeded warning
Proclaiming the midnight pain.

    Swifter than eagles' flight,
    Swifter than thought,
    Death shatters the quiet night.
    O human drought....

Think how the storm gathered, clouds
Black like the clotted blood,
How the aerial highways were roads
For mad young gods to stride.

Swifter than swiftest sight
Of fear-sped feet,
Death shatters the quiet night,
O human drought....

Think of the pale child dreaming unaware
Of the sudden crucifixion,
Of the women in uneasy shelter there
From the unholy vision.

As the invisible blight
Condemns the harvest,
So death has made mute
The voice of the sweetest.

See the apocalypse of Time,
Hour-glass become iron,
See how the careless dream
Congeals and goes rotten.

When the young innocence
Knew no consummation,
Death learned to advance
The corrupting secretion.

Pain now exacts toll from the suppliant hands,
Repeats the unheeded warning,
We cannot forget in beleaguered lands
Wasted cities by morning.

EMMANUEL LITVINOFF

33. LONDON, 1940

Lonely now this unreal city of
desperate hopes and slow insidious
will to continue living, and broken the pavement
where our young desires went courting.

Low and determined the voices, like rain
on the splintered window, heavy as these
iron shutters the faces of those seeking
an end to the chain, the vision.

For those the strong, the powerful, not
realizing as yet their power, and also
for these, the impotent, let mastery be given
and the will to act, that out

of this, the Indescribable, treading
the path of promises, hope shall fuse,
resolve spring as ears to reaper, sharper
than this, fertile as those.

ALAN ROOK

IV. *In Memoriam*

34. IN MEMORIAM—P.W.

Just as the flower of life seemed set to bloom
And as the sun had pierced a frigid sky,
You chose the solemn, unrelenting tomb,
You chose to die.

Though Winter's cares were now sad memories,
Though birds, who fled from English snow,
Gave us once more their gold-toned melodies,
You thought to go.

What dull dismay, what swiftly-formed despair,
Set you upon your undiscerning course?
A harrowed mind? A heart too full of care?
The madness of remorse?

For laughter, friends, the joy of spring's array,
For the first red streak in a hard-protesting cloud,
Heralding dawn, and the start of a summer's day
You took a shroud.

Now, you've left the flower-decked fields of home,
The garden where you loved to stroll alone
And count the violet gentians in the loam,
One by one;

Now, you see, by wisdom learned in death,
That all things pass as the wind's soft-winged caress
And passions, fading into nature's endless breath,
Leave no wilderness.

But if you feel you left the field too soon;
Now leaderless, the men you should have led,
Still are a smile, and, one drear afternoon,
Kindness remembered.

PETER BAKER

35. COLD, COLD, COLD

White May in our moonlit trysting place
    Where the quiet dead lie long;
Drift of your hair across my face;
    In my heart an old, mad song.

'Diarmuid slept, with but stars above;
    Sleepless Grania sighed
And bared her breast in her urgent love,
    And loosed her hair's dark tide.

    "Know ye not years may mar the young;
        What is unbroken bread?
    What can I bring the honey of tongue to tongue,
        That each by each be fed?"

Diarmuid woke, and the stars were clear,
    And the night was very still:
"Broken the bread we shall leave here."
    White peace came down on the hill.'

It is May again, but the dead lie lone;
    Your tresses are coifed with care;
The heart in my breast is cold as stone...
    Would God with the dead I were.

PATRICK BYRNE

36. CROCUS BUD ON A LOVER'S GRAVE

Rise, crocus, on that dew bedampened place
Where now she lies whose body's earthly dust
Nurtures your beauty that alone respects her grace
Whose face to yours was gold to rust
Whose kindliness was love to lust.

35

Come, crocus, with your petal lips tight pressed
Boast your maturity and part them wide
As once she hers, until my tongue did rest
Against her teeth and blessed her virgin pride
And watched her as she fell asleep and died.

O, crocus, from that love-rich soil arise
Burst forth your splendour and outgrow your size
Till as a tulip you can full defy the earth
And miracles may pay their homage to her worth
Tears from those weeping eyes
As sap within your stem do rise.

Petals, what promise can you not provide
Who art her frame new-fashioned forth from earth,
Who art her fingers and her ears who died,
Whose scent is but her reincarnate breath,
Whose beauty but defiance of her death?

TIMOTHY CORSELLIS

37. ALL THROUGH THAT YEAR—

All through that year, he, almost still a boy,
Planned, gazed ahead. Time's unsuspected slope
Hooded the sails of gladness and of hope,
As the glass bottle does the full-rigged toy.

This snapshot taken soon before he died—
The smile, the eager look we so well knew—
Perplexes us: we are like children who
Wonder: *How did the tall sails get inside?*

N. K. CRUICKSHANK

38. ELEGY

(*In Memoriam—June* 1941, R. R.)

Friend, whose unnatural early death
In this year's cold, chaotic Spring
Is like a clumsy wound that will not heal:
What can I say to you, now that your ears
Are stoppered-up with distant soil?
Perhaps to speak at all is false; more true
Simply to sit at times alone and dumb
And with most pure intensity of thought
And concentrated inmost feeling, reach
Towards your shadow on the years' crumbling wall

I'll say not any word in praise or blame
Of what you ended with the mere turn of a tap;
Nor to explain, deplore nor yet exploit
The latent pathos of your living years—
Hurried, confused and unfulfilled,—
That were the shiftless years of both our youths
Spent in the monstrous mountain-shadow of
Catastrophe that chilled you to the bone:
The certain imminence of which always pursued
You from your heritage of fields and sun....

I see your face in hostile sunlight, eyes
Wrinkled against its glare, behind the glass
Of a car's windscreen, while you seek to lose
Yourself in swift devouring of white roads
Unwinding across Europe or America;
Taciturn at the wheel, wrapped in a blaze
Of restlessness that no fresh scene can quench;
In cities of brief sojourn that you pass
Through in your quest for respite, heavy drink
Alone enabling you to bear each hotel night,

Sex, Art and Politics: those poor
Expedients! You tried them each in turn,

With the wry secret smile of one resigned
To join in every complicated game
Adults affect to play. Yet girls you found
So prone to sentiment's corruptions; and the joy
Of sensual satisfaction seemed so brief, and left
Only new need. It proved hard to remain
Convinced of the Word's efficacity; or even quite
Certain of World-Salvation through 'the Party Line'....

Cased in the careful armour that you wore
Of wit and nonchalance, through which
Few quizzed the concealed countenance of fear,
You waited daily for the sky to fall;
At moments wholly panic-stricken by
A sense of stifling in your brittle shell;
Seeing the world's damnation week by week
Grow more and more inevitable; till
The conflagration broke out with a roar,
And from those flames you fled through whirling smoke,

To end at last in bankrupt exile in
That sordid city, scene of *Ulysses*; and there,
While War sowed all the lands with violent graves,
You finally succumbed to a black, wild
Incomprehensibility·of fate that none could share....
Yet even in your obscure death I see
The secret candour of that lonely child
Who, lost in the storm-shaken castle-park,
Astride his crippled mastiff's back was borne
Slowly away into the utmost dark.

DAVID GASCOYNE

39. THE BIRD

I

A bird flew tangent-wise to the open window,
His face was a black face of black, unknowing death;
His eyes threw the grim glint of sharpened stones
That children pile by unfrequented roads.

And that night, dreaming into a rapture of cardboard
    life,
I started at the lean face of the bird;
A crow I think it was; but it was also death:
And sure enough there was the crisp telegram next
    morning.

I placed my mirror to the flat, unfiltered light,
But the razor cut me, in spite of the guarantee;
And I knew it was not the razor, but the ebony beak,
That slashed the base of my left nostril.

II

I loved the man who lay in the cheap coffin.
It was he first showed me the damp, stereoscopic fields
Of County Down; and now he was away to farm
The curving acres of his jealous God.

I loved the ploughing of his sun-caught brow,
And the haylines and chicken-feathers in his hair,
That was hay itself; the strongly cobbled boots,
And the swaying, coloured idiom of his mind.

And now he was lying with the Holy Bible under his
    chin,
Sorry only to have died before harvest and turf-cutting:
Lying dead in the room of rafters and the gray, stopped
    clock—
Because of the hatred of the bird I did not kill.

Sometimes now, years after, I am nakedly afraid in
    mid-winter,
And ashamed to be afraid of an incessant beak,
That raps a symphony of death on the window-panes,
Of the window I dare not throw wide open.

But one evening, just before I go to bed to die,
There will be the black face of black, unknowing death,
Flying past my open window; there will be the black bird,
With poison in his beak, and hatred in his wings....

ROBERT GREACEN

40.   REQUIEM

    (For GRANVILLE CRAIG)

Calamity has befallen our house. One who is dear is dead.
Withered and dried his eyes, and quiet his dear head.

The toy on the mantelpiece and the dog in the matchbox
Share the air that he breathed at this tragic moment.

All the world is still, which his bitterness humbled,
All but music is dumb, and hushed all the humdrum,

While the saddest waltz is played. O Death has fallen
Harsh on our house, and puts its hand to our garden.

Sorrow our song and tears, the snow on the tree.
Life is a jest at best, death the one known mercy.

NICHOLAS MOORE

41.   DEATH OF A HERO

Not here, among the scenes he loved, to die,
   But far away, 'neath the blood-red sky of dawn,
The soul that once was turbulent will fly
   Into the greater space, to seek a morn

40

Less fearful than it knew of old. The sound
   Of Battle will grow dim into his ears,
And then they'll come and bury in the ground
   The last of him...the last...the last; and fears
He will not know, nor joy, nor quickening mind,
   Nor feel his limbs bathed in the morning dew;
His vacant eyes will stare as if to find
   Somewhere in the gloom the eyes of you....

And you will not be there (and this last pain
Will hurt him most...will rend his heart again).

PAUL SCOTT

42. THE UNKNOWN WARRIOR SPEAKS

You who softly wane into a shadow,
Whom long night-winds have gently trampled by,
Who pick all flowers that you wish from meadows,
Who think and dream and sing,
And undespairing swing
To lifelessness—
You sleep forgotten when you die.

My dreams were pushed at noon into a gun;
My songs were bombs, and human blood my river;
And fighting I was hurled towards the sun
For liberty and you.
But at that moment grew
A loveliness in death,
For I have life forever.

MARGERY SMITH

43. WAR WIDOW

I can have no speech with them
When they grope at me with softness
Of lip motions thudding against thick glass.
Tears, they are born from torn places;
There is no pain, for I have tried to cry.

41

He is with me still.
The years have cast up and drifted out again;
And the memories, dried on the shore, have been
    bundled and stored
For this time,
For this quiet, quiet while of aloneness.

BERTRAM WARR

44. POETS IN TIME OF WAR
(*In Memory of* WILFRED OWEN)

Poets, who in time of war
Divide in visionary horror
Soul's dream from body's mission;
Knowing a holier connection
Than the will to destruction
Compelling the boy in arms to kill his brother:

All who tell the grave story
Of love, the sad essentiality
Of pain, whom no bitterness
Bars from life's true loveliness,
Whose words are a tenderness
Of hands, caressing wards of maimed humanity:

Spirits who dream and move onward,
Leaving to us your dreams gathered
And resounding forever in the air
O, believe us, this bodily despair
Stuns not our spirits, for there,
Serenely, our visionary heritage has flowered.

BERTRAM WARR

45. TO THE UNFORGOTTEN DEAD

Bury them deeper, deeper. The shallow earth,
Sodden with rains of winter, cannot hold
The groping hands that reach out from the mould,
The dead, that never cease to strive for birth.

42

Long since I buried the dead, who will not rest.
Nor can I rest, while those dead voices cry,
Cry in the cave of winter echoingly.
Long since I buried the dead, unprayed-for, unblest;
Now there can be no blessing for them or me.
The past is over and lives for evermore;
They weep in death who wept in life before,
In voices of wind and water and rain and sea.
They break that peace my heart so hardly found;
They would be still if frost would bind the ground.

E. D. YOUNG

46. IN MEMORIAM
    (TIMOTHY CORSELLIS, killed flying)

You wished to be a lark, and, as the lark, mount singing
To the highest peak of solitude your soul had found,
You wished to fly between the stars and let your song
Shower down to earth in gleaming falls of sound.

A century ago you might have done all this:
Flowers at your music would have set the earth on
        fire,
Mountains retained it in their hearts of rock,
In poplar boughs winds paused at your wild lyre.

World chaos coiled about you, and each upward flight
Meant struggling with the deep morass of history:
Luck was against you, poet, that you lived when guns
And tramping feet was all that mankind knew of poetry.

But solitude still called—you became an eagle.
Beneath your wings you held the slanting clouds of gold,
The earth seemed now a comic tune, for mighty
        orchestras
Drew you towards the sun, unblinded, bold.

A letter tells us you are dead—at twenty years.
From shocked and nerveless hands the paper slips.
We see it all—the failing engine, the numb fingers
    clutching,
The instantaneous fear, distorted lips,

The starting eyes, the whirling, humming sky,
The sweat of agony, the bleeding fist, the flash
Of life and panoramic view before your mind,
The whistling, screaming, downward rush, the crash.

The grass, the lonely hills, are weeping tears of green,
The sky bends low, embracing in a gentle shroud of air
Your shattered body; and the wind that sweeps the
    waves
Is mourning for your lively eyes and thick locks of your
    hair.

We, your friends, will not give way to alien tears,
But we shall think in firelight of your grave voice reading
    verse,
Remember all your wit, your poses, and your heart
Far kinder than you'd ever have us guess.

Come! let us dance in nightclubs you frequented,
Covet with envious eyes half-breeds you wished to gain,
Thrust our hands deep in golden hair you loved to touch,
Drink till your memory ferments within our brain.

The band is changing tune to the century's Blues:
Go on, yes, dance, I'll come when I am needed—
On a far hill a youth *lies* dead, his mouth towards the mud,
And, like the blood, his *song* dissolves in earth,
    unheeded.

Play on, O Harlem band, O swing *your* blues!
Rend every stone with your terrible, *lamenting* cry:
Those who would sing of life, and hope, *and* joy,
Are driven out to hunt, to kill, to die.

PATRICIA LEDWARD

44

V. Songs in Wartime

47. WARTIME LOVE-SONG

The wind sings for you
the grass echoes his longing
in a million fluted rustles
a bladed symphony
unspoken prayers
nature's supplication
to the merciless gods of war

they have torn you from me
and we undefended feel
our voices fall about us in endless confusion;
amorous phrases rebound broken
on an inanimate universe.

The winds that call for you
the skies that watch us with pity
the trees whose rustle of war
beseeches the gods reunite us,
all these have no knowledge
that we can
discover ourselves in their voices.

In the dead night's silence you are speaking
And from the mouths of the stars comes dropping my
    answer.

PETER BAKER

48. FEAR OF THE EARTH

In these cold evenings, when the rain
streams, and the leaves stand closer, shuffling feet,
the woods grow perilous. They are hungry, the trees,
eavesdropping, sending long shoots to tap the pane.

I can hear you, root under my hearthstone moving,
white fingers, longer since yesterday, nearer
the marrow. In these evenings
the soil leans closer, stones quietly jostle.

I can hear you, under my foot bending
your strange finger. I have heard
cold fruits of my flesh plotted, soft globes swaying,
have known of my skin a leaf foreshadowed.

The captive roses chuckle under the hedge—
the celandine is innocent. Underneath
her finger fumbles eyeholes. Every petal
speaks man not hardy nor perennial.

The trees grow perilous. The hungry dandelion
should not remain at large in our terrible garden.

ALEX COMFORT

49. SET ON THE AUTUMN HEAD

Set on the autumn head
of the red forests, the town
sprawls upon leaf and blade
but cannot keep them down—

though stones cover the seed
the root journeying under
carries the pregnant bud
and the weed in its hooked finger.

though pavements level and white
batten the green wave down,
under the wheels and feet
there flows the ancient corn:

and he for whom in dreams
those buried autumns wheel
has seen their coming flame
leap through the crumbling wall.

ALEX COMFORT

50. FOR SLEEPING NOW

Sleep in this land, this tomb:
and do not you, O watcher, seek to recover
seas that are not the same
nor can be ever.

Follow no more the harbour,
mistrust the gull whom the wind snatches
over your head, whose laughter
blows on the marshes:

shut your ears to the waves,
do what you will, so that you sleep, not harrow
the fallow of former lives.
You shall not follow.

Sleep, and in sleeping find
white arms of land on level waters riding—
turn of the glass, the cloud
the thin shore guarding.

Seas where the curious cloud
floats safely, unwatched by frightened children—
slim wings on the sun spread
mirror not the falling.

47

Sleep. Do not argue again
with puppets empty and dutiful, marching
as lean fear tweaks the string.
Seek no more speaking.

Sleep in this land, this tomb.
When the mind wakes, no travellers listen.
The heart dead is that same
you cannot chasten.

ALEX COMFORT

51. CAPTION FOR ONE'S OWN PHOTOGRAPH

A secret map is all that others see.
I, the sole native of the country, find
The skies of a lost season: river, tree,
Mountain—a vast, dim landscape of the mind.

N. K. CRUICKSHANK

52. SONG FOR A FAILURE

The lady weds for ground and grange
The lord for carriage and deportment
The passé playboy for a change
The Turk to vary his assortment
The incautious swain weds when he must
The light of love when she gets caught
  But the fool loves for love alone
  And takes no thought.

The nouveau-riche seeks poise and polish
Embarrassed Dukes snatch pork and pounds
The pretty Deb's sold by her mother
The embittered spinster goes the rounds
The pompous prelate as a gesture
Chooses to please his congregation
  But the fool loves for love alone
  And risks damnation.

The Emperor weds to save his people
The rogue to save his situation
The gigolo takes fat and forty
To reach a higher social station
The actress weds to gain attention
The registrar to license passion
     But the fool who loves for love alone
     Is out of fashion.
JOCK CURLE

53. SPRING MCMXL

London Bridge is falling down, Rome's burnt and
     Babylon
The Great is now but dust; yet still Spring must
Swing back through Time's continual arc to earth.
Though every land become as a black field
Dunged with the dead, drenched by the dying's blood,
Still must a punctual goddess waken and ascend
The rocky stairs, up into earth's chilled air,
And pass upon her mission through those carrion ranks,
Picking her way among a maze of broken brick
To quicken with her footsteps the short sooty grass
     between;
While now once more their futile matchwood empires
     flare and blaze
And through the smoke men gaze with bloodshot eyes
At the translucent apparition, clad in trembling nascent
     green,
Of one they still can recognize, though scarcely
     understand.
DAVID GASCOYNE

La fontaine n'a pas tari
Pas plus que l'or de la paille ne s'est terni.
Regardons l'abeille
Et ne songeons pas a l'avenir....

(Apollinaire)

...Then let the cloth across my back grow warm
Beneath such comforting strong rays! new leaf
Flow everywhere, translucently profuse,
And flagrant weed be tall, the banks of lanes
Sprawl dazed with swarming lion-petalled suns,
As with largesse of pollen-coloured wealth
The meadows; and across these vibrant lands
Of Summer-afternoon through which I stroll
Let rapidly gold glazes slide and chase
Away such shades as chill the hillside trees
And make remindful mind turn cold....

                                    The eyes
Of thought stare elsewhere, as though skewer-fixed
To an imagined sky's immense collapse;
Nor can, borne undistracted through this scene
Of festive plant and basking pastorale,
The mind find any calm or light within
The bone walls of the skull; for at its ear
Resound recurrent thunderings of dark
Smoke-towered waves rearing sheer tons to strike
Down through To-day's last dyke. Day-long
That far thick roar of fear thuds, on-and-on,
Beneath the floor of sense, and makes
All carefree quodlibet of leaves and larks
And fragile tympani of insects sound
Like Chinese music, mindlessly remote,
Drawing across both sight and thought like gauze
Its unreality's taut haze.

                                    But light!
O cleanse with widespread flood of rays the brain's
Oppressively still sickroom, wherein brood
Hot festering obsessions; and absolve
My introspection's mirror of such stains
As blot its true reflection of the world!
Let streams of sweetest air dissolve the blight
And poison of the News, which every hour
Contaminates the aether.

                            I will pass
On far beyond the village, out of sight
Of human habitation for a while.

Grass has an everlasting pristine smell,
On high, sublime in his bronze ark, the sun
Goes cruising across seas of silken sky.
In fields atop the hillside, chestnut trees
Display the splendour of their branches piled
With blazing candle burdens.—Such a May
As this might never come again....

                            I tread
The white dust of a weed-bright lane; alone
Upon Time-Present's tranquil outmost rim,
Seeing the sunlight through a lens of dread,
While anguish makes the English landscape seem
Inhuman as the jungle, and unreal
Its peace. And meditating as I pace
The afternoon away, upon the smile
(Like that worn by the dead) which Nature wears
In ignorance of our unnatural tears,
From time to time I think; How such a sun
Must glitter on their helmets! How bright-red
Against this sky's clear screen must ruins burn....

How sharply their invading steel must shine!

DAVID GASCOYNE

55. 'SURELY THE DREAMS'—

Surely the dreams we take
   To that eventual sleep,
Will find the power to break
   The darkness death may keep?

Surely the songs we sing
   In that last songless land,
Will be so sweet, to bring
   The dead to understand?

Surely this love we know
   Will not betray our trust;
Burn on as brightly though
   Our lively limbs are dust?

Though there's no answering,
   These are the hopes we keep:
Soft songs for comforting
   Children before they sleep.

DOUGLAS GIBSON

56. INSENSIBILITY

Death is not in dying,
But the unfeeling
Heart when the winds are crying;
Is a cancer, stealing
Over the bright eyes, glazing
That mirrored plunder,
Once a bright flame, blazing
The world's true wonder.

Death is not in dying,
But in foregoing
Beauty: the white clouds flying,
The swift tides flowing,

That is the real death, leaving
The heart unstirred,
Feeling no pain of grieving,
No singing bird.

DOUGLAS GIBSON

57. WALKING TO WESTMINSTER

In autumn London's aloud with wind, and I
Walk into Westminster along a tunnel
Of excitable leaves, a roaring cylinder
Of monotonous music and wildly magical
Harmonies of weather. Perhaps, being born

In this bewildering season, having taken
Into my hair some element of anger—
September like a sabre into my hand—
I too am billowed a folio and fellow
Of wind over this city. See, a gust

Swings me to water, spins me to the height
Of a bird's passage, or round a monument
Whirls me in the whisper of bright stone.
Worlds burn in my skull, my ribs receive
The fury of nature on them. This flight must lead

Finally to the fire and famous centre
Of all political passion. Oh there I hang
Poised on incalculable winds, uncertain only
Whether to plunge down history or climb
Into the still and bird-infested air.

JOHN HALL

58. NOCTURNE

Clusters of spongy clouds quietly
  Sidle across the star-shot sky—
A sepia silhouette against the Prussian blue,
  Hovering like a shroud above the glistening dew.

53

The warm air buzzes with silken
  Silence; the dim shadows lengthen:
A screech-owl rends the velvet night
  And flustered, flapping bats wheel down in fright.

Disturbed by this cacophony,
  The dozing earth-shy clouds hastily
Disperse, and a calico moon
  Tumbles from her ashen-grey cocoon.

Once more the universe is all on show:
  Time ticks on, nor fast, nor slow;
The heavens dissolve to pinkish-grey, the pale stars
    wane,
  The sun seeps through, and it is day again.

IVAN HARGRAVE

59. TO THE THAMES

Wind slowly down the hills
Licking the roots of willows;
Laugh gently up backwaters
And meander in cool meadows.
Empires and emperors' bones
And the dust of kings
Lie restless in your depth,
No more to you than stones.
Man lifted his hand,
Across your ragged length
Threw bridges, locks, weirs,
But never tamed your strength.

Ripple upon ripple,
Generation upon generation
Man is suckled, is ripped
From time's nipple;

His revolutions fail their promise
And you have seen his tomorrows
Become yesterdays
With all their sorrows;
Have seen him shoot, murder,
Burn violence in his heart
For creeds you knew would die
And you have smiled, apart.

You have time beat, my friend,
Buried in your black mud
And sweating among the hills
To pay you tribute.
You can afford to bend
Your path, to meander, to accept.
If man could too, he would
Be strong as time, would not lend
One hand to evil and one to good;
But plan a new eternity
And chase time
Into the hills again.

MARK HOLLOWAY

60. THE NEUTRAL

As I was walking in the Park
I met a blackbird sleek and dark
Who on a rhododendron bush
Warbled to a missel-thrush.
He preened and sang unbridled, for
He cared no whit about the war.

No thought of rationing or raid
Occurred to mar his serenade,
And politicians were to him,
I knew, superfluous and grim.
He honed his beak for an encore;
He cared no whit about the war.

WRENNE JARMAN

61. MATURITY

Once the wind was a gray-eyed companion
Who lifted me up in his arms to an undefiled
Summit of dreams, and I saw, far below me, the earth
As a shimmering pin-point—astonishing world of a
   child.

Grass whispered tales to the child as she lay
Hour after hour with her face to the sky:
Flowers fingered her pale-flaxen hair and her ears
Held the lonely call of the sea and of birds wheeling by.

A house was a jungle of·miracles, wonder and fear:
Behind every door and in cupboards were things without
   name
Who were gentle or frightful: at night mighty horses
   with wings
Went galloping, galloping wildly on pathways of flame.

Only rare people lived in this vivid and innocent world,
They moved with a rustling of leaves, vague as dusk
   was their form;
One had a face like a tree, a voice like a river,
Another had lingering hands and a cheek that was warm.

Illusion's bright candle grew dim, it flickered, went out,
Snuffed by the monster, experience, with multiple bodies
   and heads,
Now a boy with lips like the dawn, a girl who embraced
   a lament,
A man with a crucified mouth and a forehead that bled,

A woman with eyes like blue stones, a man who held
   god in his hands—
People came whirling in storms through her brain and
   her heart,
And always the cry of a fatal disaster grew loud,
Till at last, like an over-ripe pod, the world burst apart.

Tears, anguish and blood form pools in the cities,
Death, like a weed, is infesting the wide meadow country
Of Europe; starvation, the rat with the thin evil face,
No longer peeps warily out from a school-book of history.

Yet at this time of decay and world labour I know
That the rose in my heart is slowly unfolding;
In my skull the sun rises, my thoughts
Must pass through the furnace, ring hard in the
    moulding.

There is nothing alive without meaning and purport,
Every plant, beast and human, no matter how low
And degraded, has purpose. I honour and worship
The light that breaks ice, makes vitality flow.

Life bears me onward—I ride on the crest of the wave,
Onward and onward—like spray leaping high
To the sun my minutes are sparkling. Let the wave
    poise!
O let it not break on the shore, or I die.

O life, life, life! it floats upon the liquid air
Like chimes from some deep bell—and if I am torn
From the light into darkness, if death comes to take me
These chimes will still waken the people unborn.

PATRICIA LEDWARD

62. SONG FOR PELAGIUS

When the rain rains upward,
    And the rivers siphon the sea,
When the becks run backward,
    And the sunset swells into day,
When the seed cracks into flower,
    And the flower folds into bud,
Man of a rib
    Shall work a wife for God.

When oaks and alders
   Pump sap into the soil,
When props and pitshafts
   Stuff the earth with coal,
When the bright equator
   Illuminates the sun,
Man of his will
   Shall hoist himself to heaven.

NORMAN NICHOLSON

63. FROM CORNWALL TO THE HEBRIDES

From Cornwall to the Hebrides,
In Cardiff and on Plymouth Hoe,
Across this waiting country lies
The temperate caress of snow.

The unloved count the stars again
Where the quick hysteria sleeps;
Symbolic on the ice-hung vane
The nervous clock his exile keeps.

Nightlong from Russia through the wood
The winds relate the eternal hours,
And lend our fruitless, fevered blood
These blind, imaginary powers.

Whilst Memory hides the impassioned past
Where the unreal centuries move,
And in this mould of war has cast
(Too late?) the radiant forms of love.

ALAN ROOK

64. OUT OF THE MORNING

Out of the morning, grey as smoke,
Grey fields, grey sky,
The sudden stroke of heavy wings,
The sudden shock of white on grey,
A wild swan flying!

58

It came so sheerly from the mist,
Annunciation-Angel-like,
It shook the centre of my world,
It broke the greyness of my mind
Like great winds crying:

It woke all colours in the grey,
It spoke of speed and strength and power,
It told the beauty of the seed—
The core within the core of life—
In dead weeds lying;

My thoughts were shattered into light,
My heart was lifted into song;
I was that sudden stroke of wings,
I was the shock of white, the bird,
The wild swan flying!

CLIVE SANSOM

65. THE NEW LEARNING

With hatred now all lips and wings
the human mind does silly things.
Common sense has fled, and reason
is definitely out of season.

In nature class the schoolboy's head
is taught to contemplate, instead
of flower pot and cactus stump,
a budding aluminium dump.

Can God that made the cactus grow
do miracles, he wants to know?
Can He that made the water wine
make Spitfires of a pot and pan?

He knows that, loving human life,
God strongly disapproves of strife
and does'nt care a damn for guns
except if they are British ones.

'The British blockade will bring salvation'
(he's told) 'to every neutral nation.
So starve them! then, their lands restored,
they'll all be free to praise the Lord.

'You think the Bible's right—it ain't
now that a murderer's a saint.
The new commandment's "Thou shalt kill
in order to effect God's will".'

And so with tanks for people's toes
the Christian soldier onward goes.

IAN SERRAILLIER

66. DO NOT ASK

Do not ask for impossible gifts.
Pegasus is a mount that roars
And tramples the starry ones he lifts.
That way joy could never be yours.

Do not dream of the hero's part,
For love would only hurt you again,
The end implicit in the start,
With pleasure muted into pain.

The little things are the happy things:
The solitary meal in the restaurant car
When the pearl-grey Midland plain has wings
And ahead all the welcoming faces are;

The pillow's ultimate remark
On a world that were better, perhaps unknown,
Where you lie in the unexacting dark,
As you will for the rest of time, alone.

LAURENCE WHISTLER

67. OLD MAEONIDES

('And old Maeonides the blind
Said it three thousand years ago.')

Others have felt this beauty into speech.
The hills that slowly robe themselves in night;
The river, holding the last dregs of light;
The darkening sea that laps the darker beach.

Others have loved before me, but their spell
Transfigured all the. world; no more we see
Things as they are, but as they seem to be,
Viewed through great poets' eyes, that see too well.

Then dare I write, without this magic power,
Who see through eyes of other men and speak
But in their words, whose strength is all too weak
To force my own view of this lovely hour?

—Yet no one ever saw what I have seen,
And where I go, no other man has been.

E. D. YOUNG

VI. *Love and Friendship*

68. R E S T   Y O U R   H E A D

Rest your head, then, and let the death come slowly.
They will not weep; rather will they tread
With feet of granite on your tired, tired eyes
And build a graveyard from your pulsing bed.

Today we die. But urge from out your throat
The horrid anger, the sad, revolving pain.
Wells will spring up and feed your trifling hunger
And turn your wounds to ecstasies again.

Ask me not how the farce will shape its end, dear,
Nor tear my pity from its hold once more,
For grief and all the evil-working junta
Will throw up shadows on the flowering sore.

So rest your head, and put an end to trembling,
Throw to the world a light, a battle cry,
And fling their hands from off the necks of others,
Sleep, go to work, live bravely, slaughter, die.

J O H N   A T K I N S

69. C O M R A D E S

The men I seek are such as mad and ill
Would not turn back; pressed on to private ends;
Shed fame and fortune, were despised by friends:
Fell sick and died
Lost on fantastic trails.

No gamblers these, who weighed each shadowed chance
—The outcast's battle or the ordered dance—
Their way not being a mask worn for an hour,
But restless living tuned to a rebel flower
Which dying shed its perfume all unasked.

JOCK CURLE

70. WHEN LOVE HAS SAID FAREWELL

When love has said farewell, my friend,
It will not come again,
Better to seek the stars from God
Or sunsets out of Spain.
Wiser, who sees the devil's host
Descending as a dove,
Than he who thinks a second flower
Can spring from faded love.

JOCK CURLE

71. A BALLAD OF 1941

Two lovers walked down a Tooting street
To the three-roomed flat at the Radio Store,
'Have you got the key to the door, my sweet?'
Then up the stairs to the Second Floor.

Put up the black-out, switch on the light,
Pop goes the gas-fire's cosy glow.
Shut out the hum and the noise of the night,
The chatter of life in the streets below.

The wail of a bus as it changes gear,
The smell and the cries of the fading light,
The raucous song of men on the beer
All, all are gone, and we have tonight.

And the man who is weary of marching days
Lists to the music the great bed makes,
' Forget your dull drab khaki ways,
Sleep the sweet sleep from which no man wakes.

63

The faint aroma of coffee flows
Like tropical musk from the kitchen door
A match is struck—a cigarette glows—
The shadows dart across the floor.

Outside the wind and the raindrops beat
And the pitter-patter of hurrying feet.

'Press your lips close to mine, my love,
Hold my fair form till I cannot breathe
Take my body and soul, O God above,
This passionate fire, all, all I give.'

'Your soft nude life beside me lies—
You flame of desire, you draw me on.
O sweet, your eyes are like starlit skies,
Your breasts are the hills of Avilion.

'Tonight is ours, all ours to take,
These are the days of eternity,
Tomorrow we kiss and our hearts will break
In the first grey light when the shadows flee.'

The tired man slept and the night grew old,
But the dark-eyed girl saw the break of dawn—
Saw endless days that were wan and cold,
And the dull ache grew in the coming morn.

Thoughts of the devils who make the wars,
Who strum the music of flaming steel.
And force their slaves to their bloody cause
Till the dead and dying the cities seal—

—Till the daylight fades in the lurid sky
And the night dew bathes the rotting dead.
'What does it matter, we all must die,
In a blood-stained field or a quiet bed.

No, no, dear God, that cannot be,
Surely you cannot stand aside
And see the world in agony;
Or do the stars your laughter hide?'

The great sun rose like a ball of gold
And the sleeper moaned, 'My love has gone.
The endless days are wan and cold.
Dear one, did I dream of Avilion?'

The milkman's cry in the drowsy street,
The postman's knock, the Daily Mail,
The last few hours of bittersweet,
Tomorrow the draft—and the troopships sail.

You fools of men—how fair the earth,
—Of gods I have dreamed, and Paradise—
Surely the devil gave you birth,
The spawn of all evil, creator of lies.

FRANCIS GELDER

72. NIGHT-PIECE

After the spools of talk are each unravelled,
When the stories are reheated and the War resolved
Into its minutiae, on several planes;
When the drooping guests of the jazz-fringed hours
Depart from the dregs and cigarette ash and cushions,
There will be the crazy song under my pillow.

Sleep my darling, wherever you are,
Lie on cement, or lie on a star,
Sleep, my loved one, wherever you are.

Sleep in pyjamas, or golden shroud,
Dreaming of drainpipes under a cloud,
Sleep, my beloved, precious and proud.

Sleep, my darling, wherever you are,
Lie with a man, or lie with a star,
Sleep, my beloved, wherever you are.

ROBERT GREACEN

73. THE POINT OF BATTLE

The point of battle where men meet
And cross the questions of their eyes
Knowing no safety or retreat
From their foul foolish histories,

O at that point our bodies cross
Blindly, and blindly in the night
Tomorrow awaits our eyes across
The red acres, out of sight.

Yet, in those fields we both may go,
Dearest, to proud unconquered men,
Succour their wounds who suffer so
Our two-fold agony and pain.

Still at that point our bodies may
Listen and hear a quiet sound,
The planet drying our country hay
And drawing the blood up from the ground.

That, that is the point of battle where
Men find the answer to their eyes;
And, dearest, our love must suffer there
For all their million histories.

JOHN HALL

74. LOVE WAS THE WORM

Love was the worm that lit me by
Hamlet and hedgerow and the wood
Where the unflinching beeches stood,
Cool and immortal statuary.
Love was the worm that lit me by.

Love was the lamp I picked from dew,
Diamond and diadem of grass,
By whose significant light I knew
Something of what my future was.
Love was the lamp I picked from dew.

History that takes away my breath
And cuts my veins cannot turn down
The wick of wisdom that has grown
Into my blood, though I must live
History that takes away my breath

And suffer for mad immoral men
What suffering men have made in time
The terrible rubric of their pain,
Yet each and each and limb by limb
Still suffer for mad immoral men.

Love is the worm that lights me by
Willow and well where darkness is
Deeper than water, and your voice
The question and answer of the sky.
Love is the worm that lights me by.

JOHN HALL

75. THE PERSONAL PASSION

Now that in history we've seen the shapes
    And shadows of love grow bright
Thrown in sharp images before our eyes
    And branded upon our lips,
Is there ever a danger under the sky
To break the personal passion of our night?

What can those clinched battalions on the plain
    Settle in strategy that we
Cannot conceive and kindle in four walls?
    What can the soldier gain
From desperate roaring anger in his hills
Destroying his home and his humanity?

For always there the personal passion burns
    Like Christ's candle in his heart,
Pure and powerful like water's jewel.
        As the uncertain battle turns
To loss or terrible victory, he'll
Stand in a high room, somewhat apart

From the mad tumult, and at the centre
    Of a still universe where
Love is his hope and hope the strength of love.
        Into that place may enter
No stranger, but the most simple ghost of grief
Whose present and past and future greet him there.

JOHN HALL

76. PORTRAIT OF A FRIEND

His was the coward's, not the hero's stance;
    Physique safeguarded him from introspection,
And changed him to a figure of romance:
    The tough was only part of his confection.

He mocked at life, because he feared derision;
    Success, he thought, could always make amends,
For having once denied the poet's vision:
    His mind was mortgaged to his foolish friends.

Pretending to despise the abject lover,
    He fell a victim to his sentiment;
And in the kingdom he could not discover,
    His passion taught him what indifference meant.

Forgive him if he feared the world's detraction:
    Temptation in the wilderness of thought
Had changed the mystic to the man of action
    And made him satisfied with what he sought.

FRANCIS KING

77. SONNET

(For PRISCILLA)

Walking alone in the familiar places,
The places where we used to go some evenings,
Seeing things in the dark, hearing the horses
Move in the field under the Tree of Heaven,

The places where we never wished to be,
Except we liked the moon and wanted peace:
I remember the wonder of your face,
And, though you are not here, wish you to be.

O, I wish under the stars near the Tree of Heaven,
On this perfect night when the black bombers may come,
The horses only have their field for home,
But I, too, wishing, may be forgiven,

Wishing to see your face, and in your eyes
The look of love that still keeps me in peace.

NICHOLAS MOORE

78. POEM

(For PRISCILLA)

Here a hand lay. Here in a chair a body
Slumped, book in hand, and you leant over it.
Hands touched the rough stuff of your coat,
And face touched face. O here, my dear,
The first idea of resting found its place.

Now in this quiet hour, listening to traffic,
While the sun sways us and the music hovers
Over this tragic season: while the guns
Boom on over the continent, I see
Amply the simple movement of our love.

For it is safe within this cushioned place.
Not that we have not noticed with despair
The frontiers shot down, the battle going
The way all battles go, but here this minute
We have our own more simple resting-place.

NICHOLAS MOORE

79. TO FRIENDS UNKNOWN, UNSEEN

Passing worlds and the space between cities and cities,
Spanned by the arch of now and those yester-hours,
Leaning arc-wise where the cold shouldered tomorrows
Shrink softly down, the shrug of all dropping flowers:

Faces still looking on, is this your vision?
Your hold on the ultimate slim white root, O hands?
That your eyes soar in rings of a bird's flying
That your fingers meet in decision towards other lands?

White brilliant ghosts, beautiful comrades,
Tricked out of our lives by the senseless trickery
Of Time and Space, the eternal round
Of maps and calendars: those tired statistics
That make us one in a million have made us strange.

We walk in singleness on lonely ground,
Our plummet line of hearts has dropped too low
And we would lift it with the water's change
And break the barriers and call you dear:
More dear than parents, more possessed than children,
Subtler than strangers in diversity
And closer than all lovers in our union.

SYLVIA READ

80. TO A YOUNG GIRL

Were you ever young
With your small, wise smile
Forlorn and tired sometimes,
And eyes born before you were born,
And the quiet way you have of standing?

Or, can you be old, ever,
With that look of wonder on your face
At the sound of a bird
Or a flower you have found,
Or a book or a word even,
And the timeless way you have of dreaming?

O, but you are
Of that tongueless race
Of poets who though never young are ageless,
Who are wise before their time
And fresh beyond it,
With your look of wonder on their faces sometimes,
And the old-young way you have of smiling.

CLIVE SANSOM

81. INSCRIPTION FOR AN OLD TOMB

And when lord Death with all his gear
Stays his tireless horses here,
Disarms Possession, Love and Pride,
And goes his way with me beside,
Do not grieve that I have gone
This my latest journey on,
Nor think, because thy love is slain,
Thou and I not meet again,
But think I go with Death before
A little space and nothing more,
Finding way and home for thee
When thou, in time, shalt follow me.

CLIVE SANSOM

82. OPEN THE DOOR AND FLY WITH ME

Open the door and fly with me
The day is dead and her prisoners free,
For the sun is down behind the hill
And the evening air is mild and still.

Money and duty and what men say,
Bundle them up and lock them away;
The stars are out: there are more tonight
Than ever before, and twice as bright.

We can think tomorrow of good and bad,
When to be sorry and when to be glad—
The great cold moon is riding high
And across her face the witches fly.

All night long in my arms you'll be
Where the dew-damp grass is a silver sea,
Till the sad grey eastern fingers show
Then softly back to the world we'll go.

MICHAEL SAVAGE

83. TIME

She said 'One day you will awake and find
That youth has died within the amber fire
Of age, leaving but memory in the mind
Of the quick and eager passionate desire
You knew'. This she spoke near to the eye
And lip of me, stirring deep longing, shaking
The answer from me. I saw the cloudless sky
Sweep on and on behind her, heatless, waking
The heat within me to her. Glad we were
Of the young sweet love within us—the lovely day,
The intimate touch of hand—the falling hair
Into our eyes—and age falling away.
    And age and youth passed by the passing hours
    Leaving us timeless in that world of ours.

PAUL SCOTT

84. FOR FREDA

More than a year has reeled and clamoured by
Since you and I
Struggled with frost and thoughts on Hampstead Heath;
Our words cut sharply as November breath
That, with a windy shout,
Tumbled the last dead leaves about.

It seems but yesterday we walked in Kew
Through copper-dripping trees and long lawns of dew.
All that is past, and yet at times I know
We have been together, in the snow,
And by the sad slow winter streams
Of dreams.

All that is past. Another year will reel and clatter down
On field and town;
A year loud with battle on the seas,
Of thunder in the cities, on the breeze
The iron birds will come, first like a breath,
Then roaring—anger swooping—then death,

Death for the innocent—but is that true?
Am I innocent, are you?
But who may say?
The coming years must judge; our day
Still holds its wrath; the years
Alone can give the answer to our fears.

MARGERY SMITH

85. SONG

If I am any hope
Your silences are lies,
If I am any doubt
It died between our eyes.

If I am any joy
Your telling cannot fear;
Do you suppose that I
Should crush or turn away?

Because I'd never ask
Unless you wished to give
Do I in hope invent
A smile where none can live?

I know that in my mind
You stay when others pass,
And entering a room
The sun is in your face.

MILES VAUGHAN-WILLIAMS

86.   WHEN THIS BRIEF ROSE

When this brief rose is blown or a leaf
Dies at the water's edge
I too remember I am life
And living am decaying,
And feel the fall of dun September saying
'You will be cold'.

I dream of sunlit days in rapid towns
Filled with a dusty hope,
Where I with others build the bounds
Of lives that prove in loving
The force of lovers' freedom ever moving
A fearless world,

Yet dreaming see my children in your face
Reflect our ended powers,
Mirrors of hours when we give place;
Creating we are dying
And waking hear the new day ever crying
'You have grown old'.

MILES VAUGHAN-WILLIAMS

87. CASUALLY AS A CRANE

Casually as a crane dips over the water
And leaves a ring of trembling tipped by wing
You smiled into my eyes and left your laughter
Till I am wholly troubled, poised at centre,
Martyred by its sting.

Each day I watch you wheel in others' mazes,
Move in the moment, lift your graceful head,
Swing the slim lotus of your body as a bird rises,
Lend your live summer till it loses
Its colour to these dead.

Startled I feel my blood race when you answer,
Or suddenly resent a careless ease with friend,
Humbly linger at your side, rebuked by silence,
Sadly find a foolish thrill of senses
I know will never end.

MILES VAUGHAN-WILLIAMS

88. PERVANEH

Your arms, my dear, are safety's shield,
Tender the joy to lie and yield.

Aeroplanes thunder through the night
But stillness makes up our delight.

In other time, in other place
I've known in dreams this same embrace.

And what I cannot easily tell
I'll leave because you know it well.

O war no longer matters when
Each thought can bring this joy again.

And in our hearts each deep caress
Is brave beyond the last morass.

JOHN WALLER

VII. *'In the midst of death is life'*

89. IN THE MIDST OF DEATH IS LIFE

Within the flower, the root;
Behind the root, the seed;
Under the casual drift
Of last year's leaves,
The frail fern-frond and the latent oak.

Within the man, the child;
Behind the child, the cell;
After negation, loss, the new desire.
Out of decay, the blossom;
Out of corruption, life;
After the ageless funeral of men,
Falling like corn, like flowers,
Driven like leaves,
After the endless waste and death of men—
Endless renewal and rebirth of Man.

Within Man, the vision;
Behind the vision, God.
Out of the clash of stars, the spinning world;
Out of the clash of beasts, the soul.
Out of the ruins of despair and time,
Unpatterned history, destruction, fear,
The goad of money, hate, the tyrant's hour,
Out of all these—the root, the core, the cell,
Beauty's progenitor, the seed of life.

CLIVE SANSOM

90. AFTERWARDS

When the grey night is pierced
By the rose-lipped rays of dawn,
And the night of nations' agonies
Makes way for ecstatic morn:

When the shell-drowned songs of summer
Thrill once again the sun-bound air;
I shall return to the hills of heaven
And hear the songs of silence there.

PETER BAKER

91. THE SECRET DREAM

The secret dream, the young hope curled
In the dark winter of the world
Cannot endure, cannot remain
Forever still. What is unknown
Beneath the whip of grief and pain,
Dumb but unbroken, and alone
Like a small seed within the earth,
Patient, enduring, with the flame
Of life within, that comes to birth
Despite the bitterness of frost.
So is the heart's bright seed; the same
Glad future world that is not lost
So long as man still dreams and sees
Beyond our little world, the power
That springs from present agonies,
Breaking into glorious flower,
The secret dream of mankind curled
In this dark winter of the world.

DOUGLAS GIBSON

The Night was Time.
The phases of the Moon,
(Dynamic influence, controller of the tides),
Its changing face and cycle of quick shades,
Were History, which seemed unending. Then
Occurred the prophesied and the to-be-
Recounted Hour when the reflection ceased
To flow like unseen life-blood in between
The Night's tenebral mirror and the lunar light,
Exchanging meaning. Anguish like a crack
Ran with its ruin from the fulfilled Past
Towards the Future's emptiness; and *black*,
Invading the whole prism, became absolute.

Black was the No-Time at the heart
Of Time (the frameless mirror's back).
But still the Anguish shook
As though with memory and with anticipation; till
Its terror's trembling broke
By an unhoped-for miracle Negation's spell:
Death died and Birth was born with one great cry,
And out of some uncharted spaceless sky
Into the new-born Night three white Stars fell.

And were suspended there a while for all
To see and understand (though none may tell
The inmost meaning of this Mystery).

The First Star has a name which stands
For many names of all things that begin
And all first thoughts of undivided minds.
The Second Star
Is nameless, and shines bleakly as the pain
Of an existence conscious only of its end

78

And inarticulate, alone
And blind. Immeasurably far
Each from the other First and Second spin;

Yet to us at this moment they appear
So close to one another that their rays
In one blurred conflagration intertwine,
So that the Third seems born
Of their embracing: Till the outer pair
Are seen apart again,
Fixed in their true extremes. And in between,
Expected forerunner of Dawn,
No longer seen
But burning everywhere,
The Third Star balanced shall henceforward shine
Through all dark still to come, serene,
Ubiquitous, immaculately clear:
A magnet in the middle of the maze, to draw us on
Towards that Bethlehem beyond despair
Where from the womb of Nothing shall be born
A Son.

DAVID GASCOYNE

93. THERE WILL BE MUSIC

After the band has gone
There will be music
· But now
Now it is only continuation
Continuation of the day's drudgery—
The machine stamping patterns out of sheet metal
And the ceaseless clatter of the typewriter.

There is no life here
Only the tuneless tub-thumping
Of a few half-cold corpses
To warm your dear hearts—
The slaves of a tottering system
Grudgingly carrying on the bad work.

After the band has gone
There will be music
But how many of us will be there to hear it?

IVAN HARGRAVE

94. LET THE WARM AIR CONDENSE ON THE
    WINDOW

Let the warm air condense on the window,
Let the drops form and mist over the view:
What do I care?

The world outside is distorted enough by now
For it to be pleasanter not to have to see it
All the time. From here
We have watched it grow
More twisted and cretinous every year
For as many years as we can remember, though you
Remember fewer years than I.

As we sit
In the usual chairs, the windows mist
Over, and the world we knew gradually
Fades away: fades away like a prophecy
Of what is to come, will come, must come—
Who will be able to resist
What is inevitable?
No, it has not faded quite:
You may think it has,
But turn on the wireless—
As you hear, the Bankers are still in Power.
Have no fear, their turn will come;
Some will fight and some,
Terrified will cower,
But the dreadful drum
Of doom will halt their flight,
For this must be the people's will—
Once for all to free the world and set things right.

Let the warm air condense on the window:
What do we care?
This prophecy is real
And portends the inevitable destruction
Of the festering, palsied world
We know, and the construction
Of a New World, strange and different,
Whose blazing flag has yet to be unfurled.

IVAN HARGRAVE

95. NOT REVENGE...BUT THESE

Is my wrath splendid? Yet I become
a heart of sorrow, lips made for pain,
eyes that see only to give tears;
anger without endurance swears to avenge
my numberless deaths; when the dead are with me
earth has no blossoming, the stars no light,
but above all, the sacrificial innocents
no consolation....

I say, I will be God, my terrible arm will strike
fire from stone, flood from the gentle stream,
embattled, I would march before Israel; Yet I become
the mother, infinitely suffering, endlessly sad;
the agony is itself, what has it to do with revenge?

Only the recompense of resurrection is just,
the whole made whole, scars erased
from bewildered eyes and the innocents restored;
O God, only these....

Not the waiting
in the night for memory to cease; far lands
beckoning escape from the afflicted earth;
not the penalty unto the third and fourth generation
upon these children; not grief in immortal measure
for the defeated; O God, not these....

Only the gracious heart returned,
the summer-blossoming soul and the kindled stars;
children unafraid in meadows, laughter
billowing from the unsinister skies;
God, only these....

EMMANUEL LITVINOFF

96. THE STAR

I see Heaven's high son on the lowly branch,
And the sun shines over the French festival of the
      Bastille,
But the sons of France have heads bowed.
I see thy crucified sons, O heaven, lying under steel,
Shot in the bled ground, or rocked in a mad country.

I hear women weeping, and their tears like pins on the
      tree,
Singing songs of the wine in Spain, the grape
Squashed out by Franco in the blood of a man,
Lorca lying under the wings of hope,
But the wings were steel, and it was a mad country.

I see a star over this rocking heaven,
And a man and a woman who are young and in love,
Watching the lights in Europe's evening
Go out like pins on the crying tree. O love,
The star turns red, and shines on a glad country.

NICHOLAS MOORE

97. PEACE

All this shall pass,
But this shall be again,
As surely as the shadows on the grass
Declare the coming and departing men,
Or as the seasons flicker with the sun
Winter, Spring, Summer, Fall, one ever after one.

World-peace goes leaden-foot between the wars,
Limps wearily between the roars
Of iron days
But in among the murder-rays,
A brighter flame,
Peace, enters singly as she always came
When she desired Eternal rest:
It is her singleness impressed
Upon a soul, a soul, a soul,
That shall in time give wisdom to the whole.

MARGERY SMITH

98. THE SPREADING CROSS

Where, where will we find us after wreck,
Deep river, sand or shallow?
After the city is slain and the thin laughter
Of mouldy bone echoing in corners; after swallow
And stick and bone are mixed in slaughter;
After the memories, memorials—and after
Where will we find us after wreck?

After the burst of treaties and brute splendour
Loud on the slaughter bleeding empty stone;
When our sharp loves are blunted like night
Forking nowhere, and wind distractedly pulls bone from
        bone;
When the pulse is slow and thorned, the lips tight
And angry fires are loading another fight—
Where will we find us after wreck?

The clouds of fear are silently assembled above this night
To disappear in soft immersion in the cavern heart.
The seven-voiced guns are talking fast again
And again and again the planes return to London. The start
This of the spreading cross and pain;
But when the floods come and doves return,
Where will we find us after wreck?

A simple book of his, the awful other's want,
A little mercy on the clean surgeon's knife
Would have avoided all this. Who can say?
Today the cars of war run only when life
Is stranded for reason. And when the day
Of reckoning descends and someone, perhaps he, the
    other, has to pay—
Where will we find us after wreck?

Life is not single or double, but like an ocean
Drawn around the earth on meeting floors.
(Movement in the local place disturbs the love-beds all.)
Hunger and anger are not indigenous, but spread like sores
Across the earth from Washington to Calcutta. But
    when the pall
Of smoke and lies is lifted and the deceivers fall, all,
Where will we find us after wreck?

These are the things we must think of. Tonight the
    bowl air is taut.
The points of flame about the plane are two angers
    meeting;
But they will break each other
And our hot anger dying
What we must love and hate or fight about
Is when the bombs and bands are ushered out
Where, O where will we find us after wreck?

                                        TAMBIMUTTU

99. EPITAPH

Perhaps only an elusive shadow
Who so strangely resembles whom I ceased to remember
Who once at night made a bright dream
Joyful with softness of arms and a long look
Saying 'We shall meet again' while parting grew sad
As the hopeful eyes faded and I knew that only
Tomorrow remained, another day to be lonely.

That was the Hamlet of eyes and hope and dream
Though not of heart. Heart chose the Peter Pan
Who wandered like a wish between the brain
And its desires. Wildly we strove
To an allotted end. Braving the other
We made our memories, which like lovers hold
Softly to evening, never to be old.

Out of a darkened history came the other
In the worst of possible places, rather prone
To admire the giant, the hero, the good at games,
Or just to be dull. This was the one
To walk up hills with or to take to pubs,
To scorn or be awed by, in the end to leave
For an older gladness and a new grief.

O the day will be bright tomorrow
For the evening is sorrow enough.
JOHN WALLER

100. THERE ARE CHILDREN IN THE DUSK

Forget the dead, this time
Who are not glorious.
Their sacrifice builds to our crisis,
And the last war left us no sites
To raise our monuments.
We will not weep at unveilings;
Tenderness only confuses
The children who wait in the dusk.
BERTRAM WARR

101. WORKING CLASS

We have heard no nightingales singing
In cool dim lanes, where evening
comes like a procession through the aisles at passion-
    tide
filling the church with quiet prayer dressed in
    white.

85

We have known no hills where sea-winds sweep
    up thyme perfume,
and crush it against our nostrils, as we stand by
    hump-backed trees.

We have felt no willow leaves pluck us timidly
    as we pass on slack rivers;
a kiss, and a stealing away, like a lover who dares
    no more.

For we are the walkers on pavement,
who go grey-faced and given-up through the rain;
with our twice turned collars crinkled,
and the patches bunched coarsely in our crotches.
They have gashed the lands with cities,
and gone away afraid when the wounds turned blue.
Beauty has crept into the shelves of squat buildings,
to stare out strangely at us from the pages of Keats,
and the wan and wistful Georgian leaves.
These are our birthright, smoke and angry steel,
and long stern rows of stone, and wheels.
We are left with the churches, the red-necked men
    who eat oysters,
and stand up to talk at us in the approved manner.
We are left with the politicians who think poorly
    of us,
and who stand back with chaos in their pale old eyes
whimpering, 'That is not what we wanted. No,
it was not to have gone that way.'
They are very old, but we have been very ill,
and cannot yet send them away.

But there are things that still matter, something
yet within us;
nights of love, bread and the kids,

and the cheek of the woman next door,
thoughts that glitter sometimes like a ruby on a
    mud-flat,
dreams that stir, and remind us of our blood.

Though the cities straddle the land like giants
holding us away,
we know they will topple some day,
and will lie over the land, dissolving and giving off
    gases.
But a wind will spring up to carry the smells away
and the earth will suck off the liquids and the
    crumbling flesh,
and on the bleached bones, when the sun shines,
we shall begin to build.

BERTRAM WARR

102. IT WILL NOT LAST

It will not last, love will again be free:
There will be one who watches from this hill,
With rich contentment in his eyes, the grey
Flow of eternal afternoon one way,
The valley bindweed in his fingers still.

There will be one who from a drawer will take
Labour and hearts-ease for the growing nights:
There will be one who kneels at hide-and-seek
Beneath the yews, too overcome to speak:
There will be lovers putting out the lights.

All will be selfish, weaving as did we,
The world they wish, the bright or dim cocoon,
The daring or the cosy ecstasy.
Sick heart, take comfort then; for there will be
All that there was: good days, though not our own.

For what's the difference, if those eyes that watch—
That hand that threads the needle by the flame—
Those hands that grope towards the flame and touch–
Are but the dream of wombs? They will be rich.
We were: they will be. It will be the same.

LAURENCE WHISTLE

103. THE BURNING-GLASS

A girl there was in a far city
Who said, 'Though Ruin's face
Is obvious now in the lanes of this city,
And Panic's woman-voice,
Coming and going in the nightmare city,
Sing I will and rejoice!

'Rejoice that in a room in this city,
When I whimpered and found myself,
I found desire in the roots of my tongue,
In the buds of my fingers, health.

'Yet when I dropped from the dusk of God,
I shrank from this temporal blaze.
I could but mew to my mother, "Alas!"
But He gave me self like a burning-glass,
And a white book of days.
And there I have burned certain words of a poem
Nothing will ever erase.

'Though all the tongues in terror are crying,
Past terror I will be gay;
Though all the fingers are destroying,
I will create!' said she.
'I will use the unique glass of my body;
I will finish that poetry.'

The city twitched like a martyr's mouth
At each turn of the screw.
The city howled and got each night
Its brief and metal dew:
Solid house today—tomorrow,
Gap the wind looks through.

O why do all those people stand
About a creeping stain?
O why do all those people run
When the dust blows off the stone?

Do arrows or do bullets sing?
What outrages the air?
Are cannon-balls or bombs a-bounce?
And who is serving there?

The dateless fury smothers all.
One thing alone is clear—
A laughing and blaspheming face
Is framed within that door.

A laughing, swearing soldier she
Lets in at shut of dark,
That from the loud embrace of death
May leap the living spark,
That no breath but a fervent breath
May fan that spark to flame;
For only those have fervour now
Who play the soldier's game.

And bold she is to let him in,
And that is to dismay
Priests who breathed a different death
In her smug family,
To shock the priests like shabby crows
That fouled the family-tree.

She dreamed that war might never reach
The raptures of that bed,
But wakened with a start because
The bed still shook, and now it was
Gunpowder's heavy tread.

The heavy hand of battle,
It groped toward them still,
And sometimes in a dream she saw
It fumbling at the sill.

O it fumbled at the window,
It felt into the room,
It snatched away her bed-fellow,
It crumbled up her home,
And as she ran into the street
She knew in terror and delight
The babe leap in her womb.

Then houses in the city showed
Like dead teeth in a mouth.
And out of cellars here and there
Certain tendrils tried the air,
And it was good for growth.

The racing vine of Famine,
It dimly waved about,
And under houses here and there
The moans and little movements were
Contortions of its root.

Alone in a black cellar
With rain-drip and a crumb,
Drop-drip from a broken pipe,
Two words, then one,
She thought that vine had taken root
Within her raging womb,
She felt the tendrils stretching out
To rack her limb from limb,

And cast about from side to side,
And looked at blackness brilliant-eyed,
Because her time had come.

'O who will cut the tearing root,
O who will ease the pain,
And take the living from my flesh,
Now I am left alone?'

'O I will cut the tearing root,
O I will ease the pain,
And take the living from your flesh—
You are not left alone!'

The Spirit of Life who fashions all
Upon a plan of right,
Who finds in agony and wrong
The notes of an eternal song,
The fabric of delight,
It whispered through the bricks of clay,
Because past terror she was gay,
And her belief was great.

And first there was a little woman
Wrinkled like the sea,
Whose candle aged upon the floor
And had a knowing eye.—
And then it was a dancing boy
Who knelt and clapped his hands for joy,
And vanished with a cry.

And then the pain was shut away
Like hubbub by a door,
And a mild ancient man was there
With wistful beard and holy hair,
Who knelt as if to pore
In pity on her face, until
He too was seen no more;

But only on her faded heart
There seemed a weight to press—
What weight, unless his holy brow
Lay there, she could not guess.
But as the wonder of her hand
Crept up along her dress,
It stirred, it uttered a low sound,
As if it mewed, 'Alas!'

How long in silent joy absorbed
In that dark hole she lay,
And clasped a shape that never moaned
But added to her joy—
What Hand was in the plaster lost—
What Cup that could not mark the dust—
There is no tongue to say.

Sometimes she heard a mingled note,
Faint *Gloria* from a choir.
Sometimes it was a single flute.
Sometimes it was no more
Than an old broken pipe that wrote
Foul weather on the floor.

She took the child, she climbed the stair,
And what should meet her gaze
But the mere wilderness of Hell
Where once a city was?
And even as she stared at it
Her thought was giving praise.

The earth was dead, and rotting dead,
But the air was howling mad.
It goggled with a crimson eye,
Grimaced and winked at her awry,

It laughed, and simultaneously
It screamed with level lead.
And she must venture through it all,
With all the faith she had.

She walked with fearful hand upraised,
She had no other shield.
She moved between the lines of blood,
And faces even with the mud
Were lifted to behold.
Mad faces cried on either side,
'A woman and a child!'

O many saw her gliding on
In a wild flash revealed,
A woman with white hand upraised
In benediction mild.
The weapons clattered out of hands,
The crooked fingers failed,
And a great shout arose, the first
That joined the thirsting in their thirst—
'The Virgin and the Child!' it burst,
'The Virgin and the Child!'

'She brings release! she brings us peace,
That the Golden Age may come!
Hurrah, the Brotherhood of Man!
Hurrah, Millennium!'
Then No Man's Land was full of tears,
But she, bewildered by the cheers,
Passed through the midst of them;

And came, at nightfall, to a knoll
On which a gutted chapel stood;
And found some sort of shelter there
Beneath its wind-discovered Rood;

And bared the pure, all-giving fountain
To the pure all-asking thirst;
And watched the soul in those dark eyes
Deep in its book of days engrossed.

LAURENCE WHISTLER

ACKNOWLEDGEMENTS

The editors are indebted to the authors and publishers of the following books for permission to reprint poems contained in this anthology:

The Favil Press Ltd. for poems from:

Here and Now (ed. Sylvia Read).
In Our Time, by Margery Smith.

And for poems from the following of their Resurgam Broadsheets:

France and other Poems, by Alex Comfort.
The Beggar's Lute, by Peter Baker.
Conscripts, by Emmanuel Litvinoff.
Song In Storm, by Douglas Gibson.
Yet a Little Onwards, by Bertram Warr.

The Fortune Press for poems from:

A Wish In Season and *The Island and the Cattle*, by Nicholas Moore.
There Will be Music, by Ivan Hargrave.
Out of This War, by Tambimuttu.
Fortunate Hamlet, by John Waller.

Messrs William Heinemann, Ltd. for poems from:

In Time of Suspense, by Laurence Whistler.

The University Press, Oxford, for poems from:

In the Midst of Death, by Clive Sansom.

The Bell (Dublin) for poems from:

The Bird, by Robert Greacen.

They would also like to record their indebtedness to the editors of the following publications for poems reproduced from their pages:

New Statesman and Nation   *Kingdom Come*
Life and Letters Today   *Observer*
Time and Tide   *Horizon*
The Listener   *Poetry* (London)
The New English Weekly   *Cambridge Review*
Poetry Quarterly   *Poetry Review*
The Northman   *Poetry* (Chicago)
Decision (*U.S.A.*)

INDEX OF AUTHORS

(The figures below are the numbers of the poems)

INDEX OF FIRST LINES

(The numerals in this index refer to pages)

I can have no speech with them
I could love Life the more
I dreamt that suddenly the metropolitan sky
If I am any hope
In autumn London's aloud with wind
In these cold evenings, when the rain
I see Heaven's high son on the lowly branch
Is my wrath splendid?
It will not last, love will again be free
I was ready for death
Just as the flower of life seemed set to bloom
Let the warm air condense on the window
Line after line, we wheel to enter battle
London Bridge is falling down
Lonely now this unreal city
Love was the worm that lit me by
Luke tells us how Jesus
More than a year has reeled and clamoured by
Not here, among the scenes he loved, to die
Now that in history we've seen the shapes
Once the wind was a gray-eyed companion
On Sundays friends arrive with kindly words
Open the door and fly with me
O see the wasted cities by morning
O that one current steady across years
Others have felt this beauty into speech
Out of the morning, grey as smoke
Passing worlds and the space between cities and cities
Perhaps only an elusive shadow
Poets, who in time of war
Related to the picnic in the wood
Rest your head, then, and let the death come slowly
Rise, crocus, on that dew bedampened place
Set on the autumn head
She said 'One day you will awake and find'
Shouldering a way through crowds
Sleep in this land, this tomb
Surely the dreams we take

99

Printed in the United States
By Bookmasters